The Art
of Coaching
High School
Cross Country

Ken Willems

∞INFINITY
PUBLISHING

Copyright © 2014 by Ken Willems

ISBN 978-0-7414-7150-5

Printed in the United States of America

Cover photographs by Roger Hagerman Photography, Marion, MI

Published January 2014

INFINITY PUBLISHING
1094 New DeHaven Street, Suite 100
West Conshohocken, PA 19428-2713
Toll-free (877) BUY BOOK
Local Phone (610) 941-9999
Fax (610) 941-9959
Info@buybooksontheweb.com
www.buybooksontheweb.com

To Grace,
a very good runner.

Table of Contents

Acknowledgements

This book, of course, would not have been possible without the runners. During my coaching years these young people were a tremendous source of enjoyment and presented me with many unique learning experiences. Thank you to all I have coached.

I was privileged to have a great assistant coach. We worked side by side for a long time.

I would also like to recognize the parents of the kids I have coached. Without the support of these parents our accomplishments would not have been possible.

Thanks to a couple of grammatical wizards, my brother Arnie Willems, and his wife Wanda, for editing this book. They are runners as well as wizards.

After retiring and moving to northern Michigan I was fortunate to get to know the runners and coach of the Evart High School cross country team. Thank you for being so accepting. You have helped me maintain a high level of interest in the sport.

Finally, I would like to thank Grace, a member of the Evart High School cross country team. Grace, I have enjoyed watching you develop into a very good runner and that means a lot. But, I would also like to thank you for encouraging me to write this book. I would have never gotten around to it if you hadn't pushed me. That's Grace on the back cover.

Foreword

As a coach, an athlete, parent of an athlete, or fan, you probably know many coaches. Only a very small percentage of coaches, however, consistently get more out of their athletes than expected. Recently, a former Division I basketball player told me, "I'd run through a brick wall for that guy," speaking of his collegiate coach.

What can coaches do to inspire their athletes to give it their all, time and time again? While you have to be true to yourself as a coach to be successful, Coach Ken Willems offers numerous strategic coaching gems that he used in developing cross country teams that consistently exceeded expectations.

I commend this book to cross country coaches who strive to be the best and to others who enjoy the sport of cross country running.

Arnie Willems, Veteran Runner and Sports Nut

Introduction

The main purpose in writing THE ART OF COACHING HIGH SCHOOL CROSS COUNTRY is to describe how the cross country program at my school was built, rather than teaching readers about the sport itself. However, in this introduction I will present some basic rules which govern the sport of cross country as well as essential information which is specific to the state in which I coached. I hope this will enhance the reader's understanding and appreciation of the program's development.

Cross country is a distance running sport. Runners at the high school level compete at 5,000 meters, 5k, a distance of approximately 3.1 miles. Competitions take place on grass or dirt, not on roads or on a track.

A cross country team can include many members so it is a sport in which no one should be "cut" from the team. However, only five runners count in the team score. The low score wins, just as in golf. If two teams are competing it's simple. Let's say that Team A's first runner placed 2nd in the race, their second 4th, their third 7th, their fourth 8th, and their fifth 10th. The result would be a score of (2 + 4 + 7 + 8 + 10) 31 for Team A. That would leave Team B with the following places: 1st, 3rd, 5th, 6th, and 9th. The score for Team B would be 24. So, Team B defeated Team A by the score of 24-31.

The scoring becomes a little more complicated if one team's sixth and/or seventh runner finishes the race ahead of one or more of the other team's top five. Numbers six and/or seven, often called "pushers" in this situation, add points to the opponent's score. But, the place in which the "pusher" finishes is not added to the score for his or her team. Consider this scenario. Team A: 2nd, 4th, 7th, 8th, 11th. The score for Team A is 32. Team B: 1st, 3rd, 5th, 6th, 9th 10th. Notice that the sixth runner for Team B finished ahead of Team A's fifth. The score for Team B is 24 just like in the first example. The tenth place for Team B is not added to its score. But, because the sixth runner for Team B (10th place) finished ahead of the fifth for Team A (11th place), Team A's score has increased from 31 to 32. Team B has defeated Team A by the score of 24-32. The seventh runner on a team can enter into the scoring in the same manner. "Pushers" can add even more points to an opponent's score by finishing ahead of any of the opponent's top five runners.

So it is possible for seven runners to figure into the scoring for a cross country team, although only five determine the basic score. It is quite simple when two teams compete and, in this case, coaches usually do the scoring manually. However, many high school cross country meets have as many as 30 or more teams competing. Computers are used in this situation, electronic chips automatically record each runner's time and place, then a computer program scores the meet.

At large meets, called invitationals, only seven runners can be entered into the varsity race. These meets typically have a junior varsity race for the remaining athletes. State tournament meets also have a limit of seven runners, but there is no junior varsity race at these contests.

The cross country season for the school at which I coached consisted of a regular season schedule, and invitational schedule, and a state tournament at the end of the season. This school was part of an eight team conference and as a conference member, competed in regular season dual or triangular meets with the other schools in the conference. A conference championship meet was held after the regular season schedule, just prior to the state tournament. The conference champion was determined with the regular season record counting 50% and the conference championship meet counting 50%.

Invitationals in this state were on Saturdays. Some schools competed at invitationals every weekend and some at just one or two during an entire season. My school competed in invitationals every Saturday.

The tournament was a four step process. The first step was the Sectional. Sectionals usually included 11 or 12 schools. The top five teams advanced to the next step as well as individuals who finished in the top 15 runners. Two Sectionals fed into a Regional so 10 teams were represented at each Regional. At

Regional, just like Sectional, the top five teams, as well as individuals placing in the top 15, moved on. The third step in the tournament was called Semi-State. Four Regionals came to each Semi-State. This meant there were 20 teams at each of the four Semi-States. At Semi-State, the five best teams and individuals who placed in the top 15, qualified for the State Meet. Twenty teams out of more than 400 in the state made it to the State Meet. The top 25 runners at the State Meet were named All-State. This state had no class system based on school size.

Many readers of this book will likely be people who have been asked to coach cross country. Others might be parents of cross country runners who are interested in knowing more about creating success in this sport. Some might simply be fans, or even school administrators, who want to see their schools produce programs that win and benefit the participants. Still others might be runners who just enjoy reading about running.

Whatever your reason for reading this book, I hope that you enjoy it, learn, and come to understand why this program became one of the best in the state.

Coach Willems

Chapter 1

The Starting Line

It's the State Cross Country Meet! Early November, light snow in the air, temperature in the mid 30's, the ground is crunchy. This is what my team has worked for all season. We're here! We made it! I know it's a great accomplishment to just BE here, but I've tried to tell them there's more. Their job is not done.

My team has toured the course, just completed its warm up, and all seven are nervously stomping around box number ten on the starting line. Sweats are still on and the starter is giving final instructions. He finishes. They take a final run-out and huddle up. Team cheers echo in the frosty stillness. There is no wind. Back to box ten, sweats come off. Three are on the line, three behind them, and then one.

Coaches have been instructed to move back, back behind the starting line. The starter is slowly raising his arm, scanning the line of runners. Gun's up! Our manager is collecting the sweats, putting them in a basket to have for the kids at the end. The crowd of 7,000 nearly drowns out the shot as they bolt from the line.

I am the coach. There is nothing I can do now to help. I know I have prepared them, but now they are on their own. All I can do is hope for the best. Sure, while they're running I'll tear around like a madman, going from place to place, shouting and screaming at the top of my voice. So will my assistant. But, they can't hear us and we know it.

My mind wanders a bit. I think about the day the high school principal asked me to do this. Thoughts are running through my mind fast enough that I smile and hope my kids are running just as fast. How did I get here, anyway?

I wanted to help and do my part. You know, be cooperative. Sometimes I think he asked me because there wasn't anyone else to ask. Other times I wonder if he really cared who he got to take the job. Maybe he did know something about this sport and saw potential in me. It doesn't matter now, I guess. I've learned a lot coaching cross country and for that I thank my principal.

I've learned that cross country is the epitome of what high school sports should be. It's great for young people mentally and physically and it doesn't cost much. I've also learned that people get into coaching for a variety of reasons and come from diverse backgrounds.

There are a lot of other things I've figured out too. It seems to me that many coaches keep the job for only a few years then pass it on to someone else. I call them Custodial Coaches. Others, I refer to them as Lifers, coach forever but never really think about what they are trying to accomplish or how the athletes are affected by their participation. Then there's my favorite, the Hot Shot. Hot Shots usually ran in high school and college and already think they know it all. Sometimes they grow up, sometimes they don't.

I think I've also figured out that the high school cross country coaching force is about 30% Custodial Coaches, 30% Lifers, and 30% Hot Shots. That leaves us with 10%. This 10% is what those of us who listen and learn can become. These people are the COACHES. So, maybe I didn't know all that much about it when I started. I could have been a Custodial Coach, a Lifer, or a Hot Shot, I guess, but I wanted to learn. And I did.

The rules, setting up and marking a course, all that is easy. That's not what I'm going to describe. I'm going to explain how my teams made it to the State Meet and excelled, year after year. I'm going to explain to you how I became a COACH, how my program developed, and how you can do the same things.

Chapter 2

The Fundamentals Of My Coaching

My kids are out there now, running in the State Meet and I'm cutting across so I can catch them at about a mile. Not right at the mile, just before. There's always a big crowd at the mile and I want them to see me. Maybe if I'm not in the crowd there'll be a chance they can hear me. A lot of things are still running through my mind, too. I'm still wondering about how I got here. How did I learn to do this job? Why do we get here year after year and others don't? Keep running, you've got to pick it up, otherwise you'll miss some of them.

I'll start describing how I became a COACH by identifying the fundamentals which governed my methods. In other words, why did I choose to do things the way I did? These fundamentals are simply common sense and require no specific knowledge or skills up front.

You Are In Charge

The first thing you need to come to grips with is that you are in charge. The athletic director or school principal who wants you to do this job is not. By hiring you, he or she is giving that responsibility to you. The vast majority of school administrators want to put people in jobs where they can succeed, if for no other reason, so they don't have to worry about it. If it seems to you, however, that the administration wants to maintain control, then you might not be in a good coaching situation. You should expect to justify decisions or methods from time to time because the administration, just like you, is accountable for your actions. But, you should be completely in charge of the way you choose to coach as well as the day to day operation of the team. Someone who graduates to the level of COACH must be in charge. Just to be clear, do not make the mistake of thinking that being in charge means you shouldn't listen to others and consider their opinions. Always be aware, though, that you must make the final decision.

While it might be intimidating for a person just starting out on this coaching adventure to debate the idea of "who is in charge" with an athletic director or school principal, it is often even more difficult for many new coaches to realize that they, not the kids, need to be in charge. Novice coaches are often reluctant in this area, fearing that some of the athletes might know more about training than they do. Or, some new coaches act like they want to be one of the kids, to be "liked." I have seen cases where a new coach had to mature a bit just to reach a state where he or she could even think about what "being in charge" meant. For whatever reason, this facet of the in charge fundamental often is a problem.

I knew a young coach who would announce what the workout was going to be, then allow herself to be "talked down." If the workout was going to be a five mile run, for example, it would wind up being three after the team was finished "talking her down." Since this type of thing breeds disrespect, the kids on this team often ran to the nearest place where they could hide. There they would sit and visit until they thought the time was about right for three miles. Then they would return. This coach was not in charge but the runners "liked" her.

Early in my second season as a cross country coach I suggested to my assistant that I perhaps should resign, that we were not improving, and that maybe I was just not cut out to coach. My assistant was a fine man, a great man for that matter, and he delivered a speech to me, enhanced by colorful language, that told me I needed to take charge. He helped me realize that some of my methods and decisions were based on a faulty notion that I had picked up somewhere. You see, I coached one whole season, and part of another, wrongly believing that every practice had to be fun. After analyzing this with my assistant, I adjusted. We redefined the word "fun." Fun came to mean the enjoyment of hard work, the satisfaction of a job well done, and the thrill of victory; not just having a good time. We improved immediately and continued to improve in the years after that. My assistant showed me that I needed to take charge and say, "OK, guys, here's what we're going to do.

Here is the hard work we need to do to make this fun. Now, let's get started and get it done!"

Years later I was often amazed at the level of completeness with which the kids accepted and embraced my methods. Two of my former athletes currently coach at the school where I did. They use basically the same approach and for more than 20 years, through my tenure and theirs, the program has remained one of the very strongest in the state.

Here's the bottom line. Youngsters want you to be in charge. They want to believe. They want to be led. So, if taking charge is a problem for you personally, you've got to get over that. You might last a few years in a Custodial role, you might even become a Lifer, but you will never be a COACH.

A third aspect of this fundamental has to do with parents. Many new coaches seem to have a fear of having their methods or decisions questioned by a parent. I'll take up the involvement of parents later, but for now my advice is simple. Remember who's in charge. Parents, in my experience, will become your biggest supporters. They want their children to succeed so they want you to succeed as well.

Being Positive

The second fundamental comes into play in how you treat people. I call this the fundamental of being positive. Kids will absorb a very negative message if it is framed in a positive way. While you cannot let a poor performance go unaddressed, it is not enough to simply label a performance as bad.

You always must have a positive suggestion to begin correcting a negative situation.

Although some situations make it difficult to frame a negative message in a positive way, it is always possible. If someone who normally runs 16 minutes runs 19 minutes in a meet, you might frame it this way. "John, if this was your first time under 20 minutes, I'd tell you that 19 minutes was a great job. But, since you usually run closer to 16 minutes, I can't say that. I don't like excuses, but if you are sick or something else is wrong, you've got to let me know. I could tell you this was an easy meet for us and that you picked a good time to be off, but I'm not going to do that either because you missed an opportunity to improve. It's gone and it can't come back. But, John, YOU CAN come back and I expect that you will."

Now you've delivered a strong negative message to John, framed in a positive way. He knows that you are upset with his time and that you will not let performances of this nature go unaddressed. Very often Custodial Coaches and Lifers will simply let a situation like this go while Hot Shots often try to deal with it in a way that is purely negative. Neither approach will produce a positive result.

The vital thing though, is this. Next meet when John runs 16 minutes again, or simply takes a step in that direction, he's got to hear about it. Many, many times in this type of situation I would wind up saying something like, "Hey, guys, John's back! Did you hear me? How great is that? John's BACK!" Assessment of individual performance was always done in a whole team setting. It was a shared experience, because after all, we were all on the same team. Runners shared one another's pain with a poor performance and rejoiced with each other when they had run well. If you want to be a COACH it is your job to make sure this happens.

Most of the discussion of this fundamental will involve kids. However, I must say that this fundamental should be at work with parents, school administrators, meet officials, and anyone else a coach has contact with, including the press. We had a newspaper of sorts in the town where I coached. I think it came out once a week, but I am not sure anymore. This newspaper employed, as a writer, a person who loved sports and often let his enthusiasm get in the way of his work. Coaches, parents, and athletes in all sports were sometimes nearly driven to avoidance. This guy knew nothing about cross country but he wanted to learn. I will admit that I did not know for sure where it would lead, but in the interest of being positive I instructed my runners to submit to an interview whenever one was requested or simply visit with him and be friendly when an opportunity came up. I also took the time to clarify cross country scoring as well as many other intricacies of the sport for this writer. The point of this story is that for a long time the writer from our hometown weekly was a voice in the wilderness, writing features on the cross country runners and on the sport itself. He was, I believe, instrumental in the development of my program, giving the athletes attention when no one else would.

I remember one year after the girls finished third and the boys fourth at State, our ensuing awards evening was attended by writers from four local papers, including the writer from the hometown tabloid. I pointed him out, thanked the other writers for being there and covering the sport of cross country, then went on to explain how the hometown writer had been giving the team coverage for years before anybody else showed up. I thanked him for it in front of his peers. After that, we received even more coverage from him and the others all tried their best to catch up. All of a sudden, it seemed, the cross country kids were all over several newspapers on a regular basis. Later, TV news and high school sports radio shows got into the act as well. Our hometown writer mentioned the awards night recognition to me once 15 years after it happened.

I was always very positive when it came to including parents. Parents were always welcomed at practice. In fact, a few actually did workouts with us. When parents did this, they always left practice with an improved appreciation of the effort that their kids put into cross country. Parents hosted pasta meals and other events. I often asked parents for advice about how to deal best with their son or daughter. Most just laughed and wished me good luck. I was always right out front when it came to including parents and, at the meets, we always had a very active and vocal group of parent supporters. Parents of kids on my team were often told that they were an essential part of the cross country program. Some parents stayed actively involved long after their sons or daughters had graduated.

I probably was not as positive with the athletic director as I should have been. I was certainly not as positive with him as I was with the athletes, their parents, and even the press. But I always viewed the AD's position as favoring sports such as football and basketball, and I was ready to fight to get cross country fair treatment at my school. When you are ready to fight, it's hard to be positive.

I'm not sure where the number came from, but whenever someone asked me what percent of my communications with the athletes was positive, I said 95%. Usually when people asked this question they had an expectation that the percent would be much lower. Many people in the world of high school sports automatically associate success in competition with negativity and harshness. Sometimes people would hear me yelling during a meet. I yelled in a very loud voice because I was trying to be heard. These folks would hear the volume and assume it was negative in nature, failing to hear the words and understand that what I was saying was instructional. That never bothered me one bit. Nor, did it bother my kids.

Now, while 95% is only a rough estimate, and intended as nothing more, I understand totally that communication with your athletes can never be 100% positive. I had to suspend two runners for behavior detrimental to the team endeavor during my years as coach.

The first suspension involved a girl who was reluctant to work hard, but yet wanted to be number seven on the team so she could participate in the State Meet. She was a sophomore with a year of experience and that was a factor in the decision I made. Rather than working hard to nail down a spot, she tried to slow two freshmen girls down by informing them that Coach would not run freshmen in the tournament.

The tournament was a four-step process, and these were the most significant meets of the season. I had the team captain address the problem and that did not help. She persisted. We were on the way to a Saturday invitational when I made my decision. I made it then because to let it go on was going to take us right up to the tournament. I informed the team that the girl in question would be running the junior varsity race that day, then miss the next two meets. The girl's mother happened to be driving the bus. She knew something was going on. When we got to the meet I informed her as well. She was angry. I explained to the two freshmen girls that what they had been told was simply not true. They said they had thought it wasn't, but had been afraid to ask me about it. I didn't care that Mom was angry and neither did my team. It goes back to the fundamental of understanding who is in charge. By the way, the suspended girl running in a JV role ran a much faster time than either of the two freshmen that day, with Mom cheering like a wild woman. Number seven had delivered a message to the two freshmen. Now they had to get faster too.

The second suspension was much more difficult for me. It involved our number five runner, coincidentally another girl. Her parents were the directors of the local youth soccer program. This girl, a freshman, went through the first two thirds of the season not quite achieving what she, her parents, the team, and I had expected her to. She was one of the best ever her eighth grade year so expectations were high. She wasn't bad, just not quite what we had all hoped for. She also seemed to be half sick most of the time. I spoke with her parents about this and they just shrugged it off. Well, one day the team captain came to me to say that number five had been getting back from our all day Saturday meets and then playing in several youth soccer games later that day. Now, this had been expressly forbidden at our Parent/Athlete Meeting the spring before the current cross country season.

How in the world could I deal with this in a fair manner? I made my decision and suspended her for the next meet which just happened to be the Semi-State Meet, the third step in our tournament process. I met with the girl and her parents. They had little reaction. I spelled it out to the team that afternoon at practice. The next morning the senior captains were waiting in my classroom when I arrived. They asked me to reconsider. They said they understood the suspension, but were not sure we would make it through Semi-State without number five. Running in the State Meet in each of their high school seasons had become very important to them. They cried. These girls were like daughters to me and I appreciated their commitment to our team. I caved in. I reinstated number five, met with her and her parents, and informed the team. Number five ran well at Semi-State and we won the meet. The next week at State she ran poorly and the girls team placed 13th, the lowest place in six years. She came out for cross country only one season after that, and her effort was minimal. This entire situation was difficult for me because the girl had little control, if any, over what her parents wanted her to do when she got back from her Saturday cross country meets.

So, you can't expect to be positive all the time. But you can be most of the time. And the times when you can't be positive, you should expect to achieve a positive result. I look back at the first story and I see positive results all the way around, even with Mom, achieved by a negative action. In the second story nothing good was achieved. My decision did give the seniors security about making it to State, but I'm not sure that was positive. In retrospect I'm pretty sure we could have made it through Semi-State and placed 13th at State without number five, and, we would have experienced the additional positive benefit of the whole team trying to step up. I had made a decision that would not yield a positive result.

Routine and Structure

This fundamental is based on recognizing that the environment in which people in general function most effectively is usually structured and filled with routine. Whether it's on the job, in the classroom, or on the athletic field, people will function best if they are given a structure to operate within and a routine to follow. A cross country team is no exception.

Our practices followed the same routine every day.

> Coach's talk
> Warm up jog
> Stretch
> Warm up jog
> Plyometrics
> Workout of the day

Cool down jog
Stretch

The practices lasted about two hours early season. This tapered down gradually to about an hour late season. There were a few days here and there that I let the coach's talk go. Usually the reason would be time constraints given to us by something like picture day, a day I truly hated because it ruined our routine. Most days the coach's talk lasted about 10-15 minutes. I always had a topic. Every now and then one of the older runners would ask what the topic was going to be tomorrow and if he or she could make the presentation. I always let them. They had heard it before. They would always do a good job, at least getting started, and I'd just chip in when necessary. I did try to develop new themes, or at least new angles, every year for these talks. Young people need to be spoken to in a formal setting. My kids got a kick out of reminding me every year that I needed to keep developing new material, but much of this information is so basic to the whole process that you simply must keep repeating it.

The warm up and cool down jogs were 800 meters. They did not take long. When the coach's talk was over, everyone would get up, usually wordlessly, captains would look at me, and I'd say, "Let's get started." They would begin the warm up jog. When they returned, they began stretching, everyone counting, on the same task at the same time. This was not a social time. We had a number of partner stretches as well as individual stretches. Partners were not assigned but tended not to change. If it started to become a social activity, partners changed and assignments were made. After stretches were finished, captains would look at me and I would nod or utter something profound like, "Yup." Then they would leave for their second warm up jog, just like the first.

Upon returning we would line up for "plyos" as we called them. High knees, butt kicks, long strides, skips, fast feet. The order would be the same every day. These were not done for explosiveness. They were done for form, and besides being a fine way to help get the body warmed up, over the course of four years I could see improvement in body control and running form. I did not do much overt coaching related to form. The plyos took care of that. I would remind athletes to bring their hands "back to the hip pocket" in their arm motion, and my assistant would often say, "Pick your pocket, pick your nose." I thought the "nose" idea was a little too high up front and often told the runners that. But it was, nevertheless, a good reminder because they liked hearing him say it.

The workout of the day would vary according to where we were in the season and in the practice week. Our staples were a Long Run of up to seven miles for the boys and six for the girls, Mile Repeats, and a workout we called "Course Sections." We usually had a meet on Tuesday and again on Saturday, so we would rotate among these three workouts, and throw in something for variety on the remaining day. If we did not have a meet on Saturday, we practiced. Workouts also often included either one or two of what we called "Pack 800's." I'll describe workouts in greater detail later.

When the workout ended, we would take a little time to recover from the effort and get a quick drink of water. Then the captains looked at me, I nodded, and they would begin the cool down jog. Returning, the teams did an abbreviated version of the stretching routine. They would then sit down and await my assessment of the day's practice. I would usually conclude by asking, "Anybody have anything for the good of the cause?" Every now and then someone had something to say, but usually not. I would then announce that they were free to go and practice was over. I always stayed until the last runner left and, by the way, I had always arrived at practice before the first. Especially after practice I found myself engaged in many heavy conversations with kids about their problems, often not related to running.

Develop routine and structure? You bet. There is no substitute. My athletes received written routines for home meets, away meets, invitationals, or anything else you can imagine. I'll share those things later. They all knew exactly what was expected of them at all times. At the end of all this routine and structure we would celebrate our accomplishments and victories among ourselves. We knew well that our dependence on this fundamental had contributed mightily to these triumphs. And we were proud of having these little secrets within our group.

Rewarding Improvement

After my second year of coaching, my teams were rapidly improving but still fell in the mediocre/good category. I wanted to develop tools to formally recognize improvement. I wanted to change things up. We now had some good runners but I wanted them to get better. I knew they could.

One day I showed my new proposal for lettering to the AD. He read it carefully, looked at me, and said, "If you do this we will be lettering 10-15 kids a year. We can't do that." I responded, "If we do letter 15 a year we will be beating everybody in this part of the state." I remember adding that if they did not improve, few would letter, and that theoretically, it was possible that no one would. The AD's concern was fairness to the other athletic teams at the school and that was valid. At the core of my lettering program was improvement, with performance in competition a close second. It was possible to letter without improvement but that could happen only if performance in competition was at the All-State level. And, there were other factors, such as attitude and support of teammates that entered in as well.

The notion that only seven should letter in cross country is not a legitimate system. It's easy, but not valid. I've had teams on which our 11th runner could have been number one on many other teams. I've also seen teams which lettered seven runners despite the fact that some of them made a joke of their own efforts.

So, my advice is to remember who is in charge. Go ahead and play with the idea of developing your own lettering system, one that recognizes more than simply existing and being called a member of a team. By the way, over the next nine or ten years after I began working with this idea my girls did not lose a regular season meet and my boys teams lost only one conference meet over a span of four years. I do not remember whether the AD gave me his approval or whether I just went ahead and did it. For sure, more than seven lettered during those years.

My assistant and I developed a tool for analyzing race performance. It was a split sheet and it gave us one more opportunity to formally recognize improvement. There is nothing new about the idea of keeping splits, but we took it a step further. Going over the split sheet as a team became one of our routines. After every meet this was done. I always told the runners that the first goal was to get out fast, get that first mile nailed down, then keep the differences (Diff 1-2 and Diff 1-3) at 20 seconds or under. The "Diffs" would usually be high early in the season then gradually come down. The split sheet gave us an opportunity to be positive and recognize improvement in a formal team setting. The sheet looked like this, only every athlete was on it:

Name	Mile 1	Mile 2	1-2 Diff	Mile 3	1-3 Diff	Last .1	Total 5k
Ryan	5:30	6:00	30	5:45	15	30	17:45

Every meet, every mile, every athlete. They were all on the split sheet. It was part of my job to see that we got this information, so get it we did. There could be no excuses, like "mile two is really far away..." I've heard coaches say this type of thing. That's just laziness. Splits some of the time and no formal time for feedback do not help at all. You might as well do nothing. But, when you get the splits, organize the information, and consistently evaluate performance in a team setting, it becomes powerful. When one of your athletes takes a step in the right direction, you can recognize this in the manner in which it should be recognized. There is nothing like recognition for improvement to create an environment suitable for further improvement. Since this was always done as a whole team activity, it also went a long, long way toward building a true feeling of team among the athletes. Some kids have told me, now some 20 years later, that they still have all of their split sheets.

I've known coaches who tried to get their athletes to run negative splits, that is, the second half of the race faster than the first. Some claim that it works. But it really doesn't. If a high school kid runs negative splits he or she did not run hard. I know that beyond any doubt because we always pounded teams whose coaches thought this way.

If you haven't figured it out by now, I'll clarify it for you. While these fundamentals require no special skills or knowledge, they do require a great amount of time and effort on your part. I guess that's why so many coaches quit before they really learn to COACH. There is something else I should mention just in case you haven't figured it out. In my approach to coaching cross country the team was of paramount importance. Individual accomplishments were secondary.

Developing Leaders

Peer leadership is just as necessary to a team as leadership from the coach. And, it needs to be consciously developed. We had two captains for the boys team and two captains for the girls team every year. Usually there was one senior and one underclassman, more often than not, a junior. Captains were not elected. Who's in charge here? Because we almost always had an underclassman as captain there were not many years when the captains were both new to the job. After the captains were chosen I defined their specific duties for them.

Often I did not pick the fastest runner to be captain. The fastest girl I ever coached did not become a captain until her senior year. I asked her then if she wondered why I had not chosen her at least when she was a junior. She said she just figured that I did not want her to be bothered with the added responsibility. She was absolutely correct and I told her so. The fastest boy I ever coached was a captain from his sophomore year on. He was extraordinary in this role and has been one of the coaches at my school since I left. In fact, both of the current coaches were captains during their high school years.

Captains had jobs to do. They got things started and organized at practice every day. They were the first step in dealing with potential problems on the team. And, most important, when I needed to understand where a kid was coming from, from the perspective of another young person, I asked a captain. They knew that type of sharing was

22

essential and considered it to be a crucial part of doing the captain's job. Being a captain was much more than leading the count during the stretches. I was fortunate to have excellent captains during my coaching years, but I also must allow that some of this excellence was developed by the environment which my approach to coaching created.

Over the span of four years the second fastest runner on the girls team was a problem. She was always on the edge. She could be a very pleasant person but she lacked the background and hence, the attitude that is usually associated with excellence in this sport. She always expressed a desire to run in college, and we did our best to encourage her, but my assistant and I wondered if she really would. She was being raised by Grandpa and Grandma. This girl had a lot to deal with. The low point was in her senior year, when the day before the first practice, she called to say that since her dad was getting out of prison, she would now be living with him in a neighboring town. She instructed me to keep it a secret. Well, this is against the rules in our state so I couldn't do that. Grandpa, Grandma, Dad, the AD, and I got together and worked it out. Later that year her dad vanished so she went back to living with Grandpa and Grandma. These traumas were only the surface of this girl's problems.

The captain for three of these years had a big job. She was a strong willed girl, an excellent runner in her own right, and usually placed third or fourth on the team. As practice was ending I would often ask the captain how our problem girl was doing. Or, I'd observe that I had noticed a potential conflict developing and say something like, "Take care of that, will you?" No, the captain did not have a big job – she had a huge job. Throughout the years that she was captain she never wavered in her effort to keep our number two runner on track.

Our problem girl never went to college, but she ran cross country all four of her high school years. She was All-State and ran on teams that placed second, third, fourth, and fifth in the State. I am sure cross country remains one of the most positive experiences of her life. The captain, on the other hand, ran at Butler University and did very well at the Division 1 level. She married a member of the Butler mens cross country team. Today, he is one of the most successful college cross country and track coaches in the nation but I am sure she is still functioning as a captain in their family. I credit her for giving our problem girl three of her four years of cross country success and I am sure her role as captain in this process had a positive effect on her own development as an athlete and a person as well.

At some point in his senior season the captain of the boys team instituted a policy of reciting the Lord's Prayer immediately prior to the start of a meet. Now, we were a public school, and in my role I did not consider it something I should promote, but I thought it was good that he had started this practice. At the State Meet, as the team concluded a final run-out and huddled up, the captain began leading the Lord's Prayer. As he prayed our third and fourth runners, two sophomores, began giggling. I don't think the captain ever knew why. He stopped mid phrase, looked at them, and said, "We're going to start over and if you don't act right, I'm going to beat the **** out of you." Now, our captain was a good sized guy and his words had an impact. The giggling stopped, they all prayed, and the two sophomores ran the best races they ever ran. That's leadership. I never even knew that this had happened until later when the captain told me. Like he said, "I wasn't about to let them ruin my senior State Meet." The team placed fourth.

The opportunity to develop student leadership on an athletic team is certainly there. My advice would be to make this development happen by establishing circumstances in which captains understand their role as a leader and can carry it out effectively. I've seen a lot of cases where captains were named but their duties were not clearly stated. You must define the role. ✳✳✳

There is a corollary of this leadership development fundamental, the inverse, if you will. I always encouraged my athletes to respect the role of captain and to take advantage of the leadership they provided. At high school age some kids are not sufficiently developed to even think about a leadership role. I always cringe when I hear a teacher or coach addressing kids who are being complete distractions by telling them they could be such good leaders if only they would be. No, many kids just are not ready. Some people never will be. That is why the inverse of developing leaders is necessary. Develop good followers also. I often told athletes in this situation exactly that. "Be a good follower!" Being a good follower involves recognizing when the leadership offer is positive, then responding appropriately.

Enjoying Hard Work

This fundamental is more difficult for me to express. I tried consistently to promote the enjoyment of hard work in all of the ways which I have mentioned. I tried to reward hard work and to provide recognition for it. I also attempted to identify and deal with its opposite, the reluctance to work hard. Doing these things immediately whenever possible is critical.

The coach's talk segment of practice provided a good way to convey the connection between hard work and success, and I made good use of that time. I told stories about my running, my successes, my failures, and I related them all to hard work. I told stories about other runners I knew and how their success involved hard work. "Hard work is why we do this sport," I would say. "There is no other sport where success boils down to just plain working harder than your opponent. You've got to be tougher than nails!" I also tried to teach my athletes that, while we certainly had opponents who wanted to beat us, our greatest opponent was inside each of us.

I know I lost some potentially good runners because I so completely embraced hard work, particularly on the boys team. My high school had a soccer team whose season was in the fall just like the cross country season. I could rattle off the names of guys who should have run cross country in high school but chose to sit at the end of the soccer bench instead. Guys who had All-State potential choosing not to run? What is this anyway? Well, I often brought it up with the team. "Why aren't these guys here? It's because they don't want to work hard. You are above that." In part, promoting the enjoyment of hard work is an attitude, an attitude that becomes shared by athletes and coaches alike after much discussion. And those who don't share this attitude? Well, we're better than that.

The first practice of many new seasons featured Mile Repeats as the workout. I had met with the parents and athletes to present the Summer Training Program the previous spring, so they all knew this was coming. I also got together with the kids about twice a week during the summer. Often the conversation turned to the upcoming workout, Mile Repeats. The boys would do five repeats and the girls four. The upper classmen already knew how to run the repeats and they were encouraged to share this with the newcomers each summer. The rest interval would be three minutes. You WERE going to do all of them. Coach was not interested in seeing a lot of time difference between any of your miles. Do them as fast as you can. There was frequently a learning curve at work here. The point is that my runners took pride in being ready to do this workout when they knew full well that most cross country teams probably did next to nothing at the initial practice. They took pride in it and when we were done with that first workout, I could see in their eyes that they had enjoyed being able to do it. And, that was only a starting point.

At nearly every practice we did at least some hard running. Sure, sometimes after a long run on a hot day, we would not, but often we had two Pack 800's to do. Pack 800's are simple. They were a team challenge and a great team builder because of that challenge. They went like this. After the workout of the day was complete and the runners got their wind back and drank a little water, I would say, "Ok, today two Pack 800's." Sometimes it was one, but every now and then it was three. Captains would get the teams organized to start and my assistant and I would time, one of us the boys and one the girls. The goals for the Pack 800's never changed. The girls were to see how many they could get through an 800 meter run in three minutes. For the boys the time was two minutes and 45 seconds. As the season progressed, records would be established, then broken. A number of runners made the time on the first Pack 800. That number always increased over the course of a season.

Now, these were much harder work for the runners down the line a bit than they were for the fastest ones. The fastest usually wound up pacing others who were going to be close to the cutoff time and I don't think they usually saw the Pack 800's as being strenuous. They were just something to be done. When a new runner met the standard there was excitement and rejoicing all around. Sometimes, if we did three, someone would make the standard on the third try. Then, once a runner demonstrated that he or she could make the time, the whole team expected that it would routinely be done. I've said many times that the best teams are those on which number 15 pushes number 14, right on down to number one. I believe the Pack 800's helped us move in that direction. Again, an example of enjoying the hard work.

I'll complete my description of this fundamental by describing a workout which my fastest runner completed. This workout was Mile Repeats. The same measured mile was used for each repeat. The course had only a few slight upgrades, but it had numerous, rather sharp turns, and it was on grass and dirt. I no longer have a record of the exact workout times, but they went something like this: 5:00, 4:58, 4:59, and 5:03. Number five was coming up. Obviously, his goal was to do the workout averaging 5:00 per mile. Notice, also, how close in time each repeat was to the ones before it. I liked that. During each three minute rest interval he would stand stationary for about 30 seconds, hands on knees, then begin prowling in circles like a caged animal, making snorting noises as he was prone to do at times like this. Well, going into repeat number five my runner knew that he had to run a 5:00 mile to meet his goal. I could see in his eyes that he was really enjoying this, that he relished the challenge. I probably reminded him of what he had to do, as I usually did, but there was no need. He ran under 5:00. The fastest mile of the workout was on the fifth one, bringing the average below 5:00. When I see this guy now, almost 20 years later, he remembers this workout and will correct me if my memory of specific times is faulty.

Coaching for the Kids

You need to find ways to help your athletes understand that you are coaching to help them. Nope, I almost steered you wrong. Let's back up. First, YOU need to understand that you coach for their benefit, not for your own fulfillment. Sure, you'll enjoy it, but if you are coaching for yourself, you are barking up the wrong tree. I've seen a lot of Hot Shots who seem to see things this way. Some graduate to the level of COACH, but many do not. I've been in many, many coaching meetings and clinics where coaches would say things like, "I won conference last year." I used to always think to myself, "You poor fool, you didn't even run, your kids did." If that is your tendency, you've got to change.

I've seen many coaches in my time. I could describe coaches who thought they were more important than their athletes. I've seen coaches who considered themselves to be incompetent and made a joke of it. I've known coaches who were incompetent but were too unthinking or stubborn to recognize it. I've also seen coaches who really were operating in the interest of their athletes, but were unable to communicate this. Perhaps this fundamental is the aspect of coaching that comes very close to being a natural talent. I don't know how to tell you to convey to your kids that you are coaching for their benefit because you just can't tell them. They won't believe you if you do. They have to be able to look at you and see it. And young people are pretty good at sorting out the truth when it comes to things like this. I don't know where this saying came from, but it is certainly true and sums up this idea. "They don't care how much you know until they know how much you care."

After my retirement I had the opportunity to assist another coach. It came about because of a variety of factors, but he needed help. I liked the guy, and I had gotten to know his kids and I liked them, so I agreed to help.

Now, he did not train his runners exactly the way I would have, but I was perfectly comfortable working in this situation. Why? Because he and I shared a belief in the most basic coaching fundamental of all. He operated in the interest of his athletes. I could see it every day. Not only that, his kids absolutely knew that he was operating in their interest. They could see it. Because of this we had an excellent working relationship and became personal friends as well. Oh yes, his boys team that year was Michigan Division Four State Runner-up.

Developing Real Runners

This fundamental is more than just recruiting. But, I'll begin with recruiting because that is the first step. Cross country is a sport that demands the time and energy to recruit from nearly all of its coaches. I taught in the middle school and I always believed that being a middle school teacher was an advantage as a high school cross country coach. My math classroom had running bulletin boards. Middle school runners would stop by to give me first hand accounts of their meets. I would sometimes dismiss the runners in my last hour class just before the others. If one of the others complained I reminded him or her how the situation could be remedied, all in a good natured way, of course. I do think teaching in the middle school was an advantage. But, the other side of that coin is that I was not in the high school. My assistant was, however, so we might have had pretty much the ideal arrangement.

Some coaches are not classroom teachers. I think that is a disadvantage but I've seen many cases where a lay coach made it work. My suggestion, if you are not a classroom teacher, is to get someone who does work in the school to assist you.

If you don't recruit you might not have a full team unless you are coaching at a large school. If you do recruit, you will still probably fight a numbers game. I coached at a relatively small school and my largest teams were really not very large. One girls team I was especially proud of had only nine members, seven dedicated runners, one who was along for the ride, and one exchange student who didn't really know why she was there. That team finished fourth in the State. This team taught me that you don't necessarily need a large number of runners to be excellent. So I had to recruit, as most of you probably will.

Recruit by talking about running. If you are a runner, let them see that running is a big part of your life. Being a runner is an advantage in this area, but even if you are not, you can find ways to promote cross country. You might never have large numbers, but you will have a team if you recruit. I've known of large schools where coaches would start with up to 70 or 80 runners and then make a conscious effort to whittle down the number. They would do this by running them so hard they either became very good (and tough), or injured, or they would quit. To me that's not being a COACH.

I had a group of sixth and seventh grade boys that I thought might be pretty good when they came to high school. At the end of the middle school season I proposed that they keep practicing after school with the goal of going to several AAU meets later that fall and winter. They wanted to. Another teacher supervised their practices for me as I was still with the high school teams. These guys finished high in every AAU meet we went to. Sometimes we drove for over three hours to get there.

First of all, doing this gave these boys the running experience. But beyond that, they got to know the high school coach as a coach, not a math teacher. This group was the heart of the boys team that lost only a few regular season meets over a four-year span, then topped it all off with a fourth place finish at the State Meet. Some of the boys were a year older than others, and the fourth place finish came in the senior season of the younger guys in the group. That meant that some of their members had graduated before that fourth place at State. One of the guys who had graduated wrote a moving letter which I read to the team as we concluded the course tour on the day of the State Meet. This became a very close group. Doing extra things like taking these boys to AAU meets is the second step.

But I was not only trying to produce cross country runners. I was consciously attempting to transform young people into runners who WANTED to run throughout the year. I was hoping to see my athletes out running no matter what the weather. I wanted to develop runners who hated to miss a day of running as much as I did. That's why I ran with the kids who were not in other sports every day after school during the off-season. I was hoping that my cross country athletes would make running a significant part of their lives.

I was trying to develop real runners. Real runners do not want to miss a day of the activity that makes them strong. Real runners do not want to write zeroes in their training logs. Real runners know something is wrong if they must miss their daily run. Developing real runners produces real good cross country teams. That is the third step.

Parents get excited when they see their offspring achieving something noteworthy. I got to know someone recently whose sixth grade daughter decided to run cross country last fall. She found that she was pretty good and is now involved in Junior Olympic Meets. Both daughter and Dad are excited about the possibility of qualifying for Nationals and traveling across the country to participate in the National Meet. Somebody is starting to turn her into a runner! Maybe she'll become a real runner later.

The mother of my fastest girl came to me once wondering if she should allow her daughter to go snowboarding with a school group. I'll admit that my first thought was, "Oh… what if she injures her knee?" But, sensibility has to prevail. I said, "Let her go. She'll be fine." She was. You are trying to turn them into runners, not put limits on their lives. Excluding certain activities because they might cause problems related to running is something the individual athlete must choose.

I knew a family, the dad and daughter, from a neighboring town. This man turned his daughter into a runner. But not in a positive way. Beginning at about six and lasting through about 10 or 11 years of age, this girl set all kinds of national age group records. She was phenomenal. I asked him about the training once and he said she was running about 70 miles a week. She was nine or 10 at the time. I was in their house once and there were trophies everywhere. Well, things changed. She decided that she was taking charge of her own life when she was 15 or 16 and her running career went downhill from there. She had a few good years and a few rough years in high school then actually went on to have a decent collegiate career, but it was nothing close to what it could have been. The point is you can overdo this.

If It Ain't Broke, Don't Fix It

My description of this fundamental will be short, but that does not mean it is unimportant. Once I figured out how to coach the way I wanted to, I never changed. There was no need to. Sure, almost every year minor adjustments were made to adapt to the current athletes, but never anything major. Furthermore, the guys who replaced me, my former athletes, are still doing things the same way, using basically the same methods and the same philosophy. Why change? It works.

I would, however, caution you to not label something as "working" just because you get better than a few local teams. I've seen high school coaches do that. Think on a state-wide basis.

My first two years were a great education. My third year I had one girl qualify for State, the next year one boy, then I had at least one team at State in all of my other years. Once I had both the boys and girls teams. Since my coaching years, the two guys who took over have had both teams at State in almost every season. There have now been over 20 years of cross country excellence for this relatively small school in a state that has no class system. Someone once said, "If it ain't broke, don't fix it." I'm sharing these ideas with you because they work.

Chapter 3

The Organization Of
My Program

OK, I made it. Just about a mile in. I've got a few seconds to catch my breath then I've got to be ready to yell. I think we got a good start, not too much too early, but for sure enough to be in good position to race. There's our first, and I can see two and three coming. Good job! Concentrate! Be tough now! Let's race! Four and five ought to be coming. Where are they?

Organization is an essential part of just about any successful endeavor. I have previously alluded to my reliance on organization, but here I will detail the organizational procedures on which my program was based.

I'll begin by describing when the cross country season really began. It was within the last two weeks of school, in the spring, just as track was winding down. That was when we had the spring

Parent/Athlete Cross Country Meeting. At that meeting I would present to parents and athletes the expectations which went with being a part of the cross country team.

One of the expectations was that all involvement in any other organized sports activity had to cease when we had the first practice in early August. I felt this was necessary partly because there were rules and we were highly visible due to our success. Once someone turned one of my girls in to the state high school athletic association for participating in a Walk for Hunger with her church youth group. She had to sit out one meet. The main reason though, was because young people possess only a finite amount of energy and I expected them to use 100% of the energy they had for sports in cross country. Remember, I had a problem with this one.

At the Parent/Athlete Cross Country Meeting I would give parents and athletes a handout with a wide variety of information. But the vital feature of this meeting was a detailed description of the Summer Training Program.

Parents and their kids sat together. I think this was important because it helped make cross country a family project. Each family received a handout which explained the Summer Training Program. I tried to keep it as simple as possible and allow for flexibility in how and when the training was done. I always suggested that the program be posted somewhere in a prominent place in the home and that came to mean the refrigerator in many cases. A training log was handed out with the Summer Training Program and kids were strongly encouraged to record their mileage. Once runners begin logging miles it becomes increasingly difficult to miss a day of training.

Did my runners all do the entire program? Definitely not. Did some do the entire program? Yes they did, and others came very close. Did all of the kids do more than they would have if there had been no program given to them? Without doubt! So, it was worth the time and energy it took from everyone. This was always the first of many times that parents would be told what an essential part of the program they were.

The Summer Training Program is a good example of one way in which I tried to produce real runners. During the summers I encouraged the kids to come to two weekly events. They could not be required, but they could be encouraged. The program was substantial but not overwhelming.

I had formed a running club for the purpose of promoting local running events and at the same time raising money that could help the cross country program. I'll provide more information about the club later, but for now, I'll just describe the weekly Monday evening Prediction Runs which the club held at a local park. The Prediction Runs were five miles. Ribbons were awarded based on the difference between actual and predicted time. No watches were allowed. So, there was no pressure for performance. Kids were simply encouraged to show up, run, and enjoy being with other runners of all ages. The local running community embraced these Prediction Runs and there were frequently between 80-100 runners. The cost for those who were not on a cross country team was $1. High school cross country athletes, for any school, could run for nothing. All the calculating to determine the winners was done by hand and I had a great group of cross country parents (the club) helping. The Prediction Runs continued for many years after I retired.

I had one boy who would show up at one or two Prediction Runs a summer. He was never there on Thursdays. Those one or two Prediction Runs would be the bulk of his summer training. As a freshman he consistently ran close to 17 minutes. Each of his other years he would run in the 16's and by his senior year he ran very low 16's. He probably could have been a state champion and I told him that. But, while it was very important to him to be a part of the team, and he valued the team's success, it never mattered to him that he maximize his natural ability. He did, however, have an outstanding high school cross country experience and, after it was over his senior year, he made a special effort to thank me. I'm still in touch with him now, 20 years later, and he still runs a road race every now and then.

I also encouraged the kids to come to the school on Thursday evenings. This run was always very informal. Some would run farther than others. We always had a good time. One Thursday I remember it was 105 degrees. I almost did not go. But, I figured I had asked the kids to come, so I went. I was not expecting any of them to show up. Four did. I think we ran four miles and called it a day.

So I saw many of the runners twice a week all summer.

The training program had three essential ingredients: mileage, the weekly long run, and the weekly hard run. Consistency was stressed. Commitment was essential. The handout changed in form from year to year but in principle it remained the same. Here is an example of the Summer Training Program handout.

Summer Training

There is one day off each week for the first five weeks. One run per week is longer than the others. That is important. All running, except one day a week, should be done at an easy pace. An easy pace is a pace that allows comfortable talking, but not so easy that you don't feel like you are doing any work. One day a week you should run at a harder pace. This can be any day and the pace should be hard enough that it makes talking difficult. Road races are a good place to do this. Do not mistake these harder runs for races. Racing will come later.

The three main ingredients in this program, in order of importance, are:

1. Mileage
2. The weekly hard run.
3. The weekly long run.

If you are a beginner do not be intimidated by either the mileage or the other information given. Everyone can do this at his or her own level. Start by doing as much as you can. I have seen runners who became very fast in their first season who had to begin by alternating walking and running. Step one is simply covering the miles.

The pace of your running should naturally get faster as the summer progresses. Your physical condition will improve by doing this program. As you invest more and more time in the process, your mental toughness and commitment will improve also. By the end of the summer some boys should be able to do the training runs at a pace of 6:30 per mile or faster. Some girls will be able to train at close to a 7:30 per mile pace. Of course, the harder runs will be at a faster pace. Commitment and honesty are essential ingredients in this program. Make a commitment to yourself and be honest with yourself, your coaches, and your teammates. Help each other do the summer miles. **Consistency** in your summer running is what produces improvement.

You can figure out your daily mileage. The long run should be at least 3 miles longer than the average of your mileage for the week. Take week 1 for the girls as an example. Girls are running 6 days this week so that averages 4 miles per day. So the long run for this week should be 7 miles. That would leave 17 miles to be done on the other 5 days. Hopefully you can figure it out from here.

Take week 10 for boys as another example. You are running 7 days during this week. The 55 miles in week 10 gives us an average of about 8 miles per day. That means your long run should be 11 miles, leaving you with 44 miles to be done on the other 6 days.

Week 1 Total Mileage: Boys 28, Girls 24

Week 2 Total Mileage: Boys 33, Girls 26

Week 3 Total Mileage: Boys 35, Girls 28

Week 4 Total Mileage: Boys 40, Girls 33

Week 5 is the same as week 4.

Beginning week 6 run seven days each week.

Week 6 Total Mileage: Boys 44, Girls 35

Week 7 Total Mileage: Boys 45, Girls 39

Week 8 Total Mileage: Boys 50, Girls 42

Week 9 Total Mileage: Boys 55, Girls 45

Week 10 is the same as week 9.

Other thoughts/information:

- Once practice starts you may not participate in other organized sports activities.

-A pair of running shoes is a good investment. Running shoes can be ordered online or you can go to a store. The advantage in going to a store is that you can try them on. Looking for sales can save a lot of money. In the fall coaches will place a team order for racing spikes.

-As you begin training it is important that you eat plenty of food and drink plenty of water. Try to eliminate junk food and eat a balanced diet. You burn over 100 calories per mile of running. That means you must eat a lot! Drink at least eight glasses (8 ounce glasses) of water a day. Don't wait until you are thirsty. Most young people do not get enough sleep. You should average at least eight hours a night. It should be in the night time, not between 3:00 AM and 11:00 AM!!

-Take a daily multiple vitamin. An iron supplement is important for girls.

-If your family leaves on vacation, take your running shoes with you. You can do your running no matter where you might go.

-Post this handout on your refrigerator or some other prominent place in your home this summer. Help each other make sure the log is kept up to date.

-When you run on the roads do so only where traffic is slow. Do not run on busy roads. Always run facing traffic (left side of the road) if you must run on roads. Remember, cars are bigger than you.

-Run with someone else if possible. That makes it more enjoyable, especially for someone just starting out.

-Success comes from commitment. Whatever your goals might be, make a commitment to complete this Summer Training Program. That is the first step toward giving yourself a chance to achieve your goals.

As summer was drawing to a close excitement would begin building inside of me. I could hardly wait for the first practice to begin. When I saw kids on Mondays and Thursdays I could see it building in them also. By the time the first practice day arrived we were all breathing fire.

I had done my best all summer to encourage the runners to train. They were on their own to respond then. Now they were mine! The first practice lasted forever. I spoke forever, and then we did the workout. The upperclassmen all knew the routine, how practice worked. But they, as well as the newcomers, had to sit through another explanation, complete with a handout, of exactly how practices would work. After the workout they took the handouts home with them. Here is an example of the handout athletes were given on the first day.

Day One

Format for every practice is the same. Athletes are expected to be familiar with this format and be at the right place at the right time doing the right thing.

- Coach's talk (5-10 minutes)
- Warm up jog (800 meters)
- Stretching (10 minutes)
- Warm up jog (800 meters)
- Plyometrics (5 minutes)
- Workout (30 - 60 minutes)
- Cool down jog (800 meters)
- Stretching (5 minutes)

Practices begin at 3:45 (right after school) and will last from one to two hours. Early season practices tend to be longer and the practices generally become shorter as the season progresses. Athletes are expected to be on time and mentally ready to practice. Every practice has a purpose and something positive should be achieved in practice every day.

Coach's talk: One of the coaches will talk about the preceding day's practice or meet. Coaches will expect athletes to listen and respond to the positives and negatives which are pointed out. The workout of the day will be described. Following a meet, split sheets will be discussed. There may be a second coach's talk at the end of practice depending on the number of things which need to be discussed and the length of the day's practice. Sometimes the talk will relate to an aspect of running that the coach selects.

 Warm up jog: This will be done in two groups, as an entire boys team and an entire girls team. The pace is always easy. Everyone needs to be able to keep up.

 Stretching: Athletes will count in unison to 15 (slowly) for each stretch. Stretching is an important part of practice and is instrumental in minimizing soreness and avoiding injury. Girls and boys teams will stretch separately. Captains will lead the stretches.

 Warm up jog: Same as first one.

Plyometrics: Just as the stretching time, these exercises are important in avoiding soreness and injury. In addition to this, plyometrics improve running form and general coordination. The emphasis is on form more than explosiveness. Exercises include high knees, butt kicks, high skips, long strides, and fast feet. These exercises are done two times each over a distance of 40 meters. The team cheer is routinely done following plyometrics.

 Workout: Athletes and parents will quickly see a pattern in workouts. Workouts will follow a hard/not-so-hard pattern. However, some type of hard running will be done every day. No day is totally without hard work. The hard/not-so-hard pattern might vary depending on the situation. Variation in distance, intensity, and duration of the workout is what determines "hard" or "not-so-hard."

Cool down jog: Same as warm up jogs.

Stretching: The number of stretches performed at the end of practice is shorter than the stretching at the beginning of practice. Otherwise this part of practice is just like the other stretching time. Coach might talk as these stretches are done.

For the first two weeks of practice, the time from which we started practice until school actually started, I always thought I had THE dream job. Families had been encouraged at the spring Parent/Athlete Meeting to plan their vacations so their kids could be at cross country practice two weeks prior to school starting. Parents were very good about this.

As the years went by, my emphasis on organization increased. I developed handouts for almost everything and with a few of my teams, required the athletes to keep a folder of them. Here are a few other samples of the handouts.

 Stretching Routine

The stretching routine exists for three reasons. 1) Stretching improves flexibility, and therefore lessens susceptibility to injury. 2) Stretching is an important part of the warm up. It helps get you physically ready for the workout. 3) Stretching, if done correctly, gets everyone "on the same page." It is an important part of the process of building a "team" mentality.

Practice begins each day with an 800 m warm up jog. This is followed by the stretching routine, then another 800 m jog. Everyone must count (slowly to 15) as each stretch is held. Teams will form separate circles for stretching. Captains will lead the count. The following stretches will be done each day at the beginning of practice in this order.

1. Toe touches. Knees straight, bend at the waist to touch toes. Right foot over left, left over right, then side by side.

2. Quad stretch. Knees up to rear end, held with hand. Right knee, then left.

3. Butterfly stretch. Sit, pull feet in, knees out. Bend forward. Partner stretch. Push down gently on the back of your partner.

4. Arm and shoulder stretches. Grasp hands overhead, pull back and apart. Right over left, then left over right. Pull stretched arm with other wrist.

5. Arm and shoulder rotations. Rotate arms, one at a time, forward then backward.

6. Hamstring stretch. Sit. One leg out straight, toes up, other foot to inside of straight knee. Bend forward. Partner stretch. Push down gently on back of your partner.

7. Back arm stretch. Bend forward at the waist, arms back. Partner stretch. Pull your partner's arms together and upward.

8. Knees up. Grasp knee with both hands, pull knee up as high as possible, straight in front. Right then left.

9. Calf stretch. Legs apart like running stride, front knee bent. Lean forward until calf muscle tightens. Right then left.

10. Trunk rotations. Arms held out parallel to ground, hands flat. Swing arms right to left.

11. Repeat #2, then #6, then #9.

At the end of practice (or meet) stretches #2, #6, and #9 will be done plus sit-ups and push-ups.

Plyometric Exercises

These exercises are a part of the warm up before every practice and meet. They are performed over a distance of about 40 meters. At practice each one is repeated two times; at a meet, only once. The emphasis is on form, coordination, and control more than explosiveness or speed. All movements are straight ahead and the motion of the arms is exaggerated.

The teams will do the plyometrics separately, and will make a straight line at the beginning of each repetition. Captains will give the starting command.

1. High knees. Bring knees up high in front. Keep arm motion straight as you cover the distance.

2. Butt kicks. Kick yourself in the rear end as you cover the distance. Keep arm motion straight.

3. High skips. Cover the distance skipping. Try for height. Keep arm motion straight. Keeping your total movement straight is difficult on this one.

4. Long strides. Cover the 40 m making strides as long as possible. Arms are "long" also. Try for height. Think graceful, like a gazelle.

5. Fast feet. Sometimes called "sewing machine" or "bug stompers." Feet return to the ground as fast as possible. Arm motion is fast also.

Sometimes the topic for the coach's talk would yield a handout. I'd make copies from magazines, things like that. Some of the kids really liked getting this material and kept everything. Some still have it years later. Some probably lost the handouts before the day was done, but the process of hearing something and reading it at the same time is a sound enhancement when it comes to learning and retaining ideas. The following handout is one that I loved to elaborate on.

Three Principles of Distance Racing

1. Never assume that your opponent feels any better than you do.
2. Understand that your mind always tells you to slow down before you physically need to.
3. Care more than your opponent.

Three Racing Strategies

Running the inside. I once had a girl on my track team who ran the entire 3200 m race in the second lane. She was side by side with another girl, who was on the inside. My girl lost by a step. The next day I measured the two lanes and found the difference in distance to be far more than step. Running the inside on every curve in a cross country race can save a lot of distance.

Running the tangents. Sometimes called "cutting the corners." This is useful when you are faced with a series of corners or curves. The term "running the tangents" was coined by one of the greatest American runners ever, Frank Shorter.

The 10-step. As you come out of a corner that is 90 degrees or more, take 10 quick sprinting steps to get back up to speed. This is easier said than done. Concentrate on speeding up your arm movement and returning your feet as quickly as possible to the ground. Some runners find it helpful to drop the level of the chin (look at the ground) as they do this.

The discussion this handout alone can generate is almost endless. I told stories about my experiences with these ideas, kids told stories about theirs, and everyone on the team would have these strategies and principles firmly entrenched in their minds before the first meet. This handout was always used for more than one coach's talk.

We were always one of the very first teams to arrive at a meet. We would set up camp, use the restrooms, and then my assistant coach and I would always tour the course with the teams. The course tour was a time to be attentive to what was being said and a time to think about how the course should be run. I used to look at other teams who were walking along laughing and shouting, chatting about boyfriends and girlfriends, and I would laugh inside, knowing that my group of focused athletes was going to kick their butts. We had fun after the job was done and a big part of that fun was simply knowing that we had done the job right.

I also had a handout for meets. I didn't want a bunch of nervous questions at a meet, so I tried to answer them all ahead of time. Here is that handout.

Procedure at Away Meets

1. Bus leaves promptly at the designated time. For distant meets, athletes may have to be dressed to run and in warm up suits before the end of the school day.

2. If possible coaches will have acquired maps of the course prior to the day of the meet. If that is the case, we will have gone over the course the day before the meet at practice. The course will have been separated into sections and thoroughly discussed. If we have not gotten a map ahead of time, coaches will get the maps as we get off the bus, and sections will be identified as we tour the course.

3. Athletes take all personal and team equipment and set up camp as coaches meet briefly with opposing coaches. *

4. After setting up camp athletes will all use restrooms. This must be done quickly. *

5. Tour the course. Identify Course Sections and see as much of the course as time allows. Athletes must listen carefully since some parts of the course or some sections might have to be discussed without being at that spot on the course.

6. Girls begin their warm up as course tour is being completed. *
   - 400 meter jog
   - Stretching (same as before practice)
   - 400 meter jog
   - Plyometrics (one time each–change shoes)
   - On the starting line (three 40 meter stride outs, sweats off, team cheer)

7. Boys begin their warm up as the girls start. Boys warm up is identical to girls. *

8. Post race: 1 mile cool down jog, team stretch (same as at the end of practices), whole team visits restrooms. Coaches will be scoring the meet with the opposing coaches and getting our ribbons. *

9. Bus ride home: Discuss meet in general, hand out ribbons if possible, team scores, etc.

Home Meet Procedure

1. Meet coaches at the course at 4:00.

2. Walk the course identifying the Course Sections and discussing them as you go. *

3. Warm up and cool down are identical to away meets. Girls begin as the opponents arrive. Coaches will take care of giving the opponent course maps and showing the course. Athletes take care of getting ready to run to the best of their abilities. *

4. After cool downs are completed we will meet at the finish line to pass out ribbons and briefly discuss the meet. The meet will be discussed in much greater detail the next day at practice.

*Captains are in charge of getting these things going and done. Athletes are expected to be in the right place at the right time doing the right thing.

Now if you read that last handout carefully, you'll notice that it referred to "Course Sections." This is something I will detail when I describe our workouts. For now let me just say that this is a philosophy of racing which helps runners think about all courses in the same manner.

Each invitational we went to had its own, separate handout. The reason for this is that the departure time for each one was unique, as was the schedule of races for the day. With the "regular season" meets (handout above) we always left from school or had the meet right there, so one handout fit them all. Invitationals are all different. I always tried to include directions for parents as well as other things they needed to know. Kids were always instructed to give this handout to their parents.

Here is an example of a handout for one invitational.

New Prairie Invitational September 19

1. Bus leaves promptly at 6:15 AM. Be there at 6:10.
2. The meet is at New Prairie High School. New Prairie is located on Cougar Road between U.S. 20 and U.S. 2 west of South Bend near New Carlisle. There will be approximately 120 schools at the invitational. There is a $2.00 admission charge and no pets are allowed. This is one of the largest and finest meets in the country. The New Prairie course is one of the best featuring the famous "Agony Hill." Our runners are looking forward to testing themselves on "Agony Hill."
3. Runners should bring the following items: Extra shoes. Wear old shoes, preferably running shoes. Keep these on while we tour the course. Keep your spikes in your bag, dry until you race. Bring four pairs of extra socks. Dry socks and shoes are a must on the starting line. Bring rain gear.
4. Wear your uniform. Bring your warm up. Wear the jacket and/or pants as the weather demands. Wear only school issued clothing. Make sure anything you wear under your uniform is within the rules. No jewelry, barrettes, or bobby pins. This is a long day so you might want to bring homework.
5. Bring your water bottle.
6. Do not bring anything that would be a distraction to your teammates or anything that would identify you as someone who does not take competition seriously.
7. The meet schedule is as follows:

   9:30 Girls Varsity A
   10:05 Boys Varsity A
   10:30 Girls Varsity AA
   11:05 Boys Varsity AA
   11:30 Girls Varsity AAA
   12:05 Boys Varsity AAA
   12:30 Frosh/Soph Boys
   12:55 Boys Reserve

1:20 Girls Reserve
1:55 Awards

Girls begin warming up immediately after we tour the course. Boys begin warming up at 9:25. Listen to announcements. If you are in a race other than varsity begin your warm up 30 minutes before your race is due to start.

Warm up sequence: Use the restroom, jog 400, stretch, jog 400, plyos, 3 40 m strides. Plyos and stride outs can be done on the starting line. Continue to be active if we have to wait on the starting line.

After your race cheer for your teammates. Get in a mile of jogging as a team. Stretch as a team.

We should be back at school by 4:30 PM.

The four step tournament demanded even more communication and organizational work. Both the running club and my wife were very helpful with these things. Items such as travel arrangements and reservations for lodging and restaurants had to be taken care of well ahead of the event. One year we had over 120 parents and fans show up at a large restaurant for the meal the evening before the State Meet. They found tables for all of us. I know there were over 120 because I counted them. I expected quite a few more than just the runners and their parents, but not that many. The word had gotten out! Many written communications were sent home with the athletes leading up to these competitions and we also had a phone chain to help make sure all of the parents were up to date on preparations for tournament meets.

No discussion of organization would be complete without mentioning the role of the assistant coach. My assistant was assigned to me my first year of coaching. I did not know him well at the time but he quickly became a very close friend. He was older than me, more experienced, and he brought a great amount of common sense to the program. He was not and never had been a fast runner but he enjoyed putting in his miles. When he died unexpectedly in the first year of his retirement it was a very sad occasion for me and our athletes.

When I learned that I had an assistant I was very happy. I've seen situations in which one coach is expected to lead both the boys and girls teams, and in some extreme cases even the middle school team, without any help. I was lucky, I guess. First of all, to have an assistant, and second, to have one who turned out to be such a tremendous asset to the program. Yes, the first time I met with him after he had been appointed, I had a handout for him. I no longer have it, but it detailed his responsibilities very clearly.

What I wanted was an assistant who would help by carrying out assigned tasks. I wanted an assistant who would listen to what I was saying to the athletes and add to it. I wanted an assistant who would not publicly question one of my decisions. But I also wanted an assistant who would not hesitate to inform me individually if he thought something I was doing was not right.

On many occasions my assistant would listen intently as I conversed with a runner, parent, or even school administrator, nodding vigorously in agreement as I spoke. Then sometimes, after the conversation was over, he'd ask, "Did you really want to say that?" The worse he thought my statement or decision had been, the quicker he would ask. Many times after listening to his question, I would hastily summon back the person I had been talking with in order to continue the conversation. I respected and valued my assistant's opinions.

Like I said, I was fortunate. But a coach does need help. If you have both the boys and girls teams and not an assistant, you need to address this with the school administrators. If the money is not there, find a volunteer.

One of my assistant's assigned tasks was conducting the workout with one of the two teams. This involved a lot of preparation time, especially early in our time together. First, I had to know how the workout would go, and then I had to make sure that he understood how it would play out. Once we got the system down, though, it became easy. I have seen coaches who know what they want the kids to do, but can't figure out how to organize it. Having an assistant makes it easier to visualize because it can be split in half right up front.

The position of manager was essential. Managers in my program usually did the job throughout their high school years. I had a handout for them also.

Duties of Cross Country Manager
1. Practice
   - Fill water container (2/3 full) with water and a little ice. This is done in training room.
   - Help with timing workouts.
   - Help with record keeping.

- If a runner requires something from the training room such as Vaseline for blisters, heat rub, etc. be ready to get it for them.
- Cheer for runners. If someone is having trouble, cheer for them the most.
- You will be able to go home from some practices right after they start.

2. Meets
   - Fill water container just as for practice. For away meets on Saturday arrive 20 minutes before departure. For away meets after school do it ASAP. For home meets after school you have more time.
   - Help set up camp.
   - Take runners' warm ups after they take them off immediately before the race starts. Put them in camp until after the race. Help runners find their warm ups after the race.
   - Take mile splits during the race.
   - Help take camp down. Make sure nothing is left behind.
   - Help runners out in any way you can before and after the race.

Shortly before I retired as coach, the school recognized the girls team at halftime of a basketball game for their regular season winning streak of more than 120 meets. All the athletes who had been on the team during this time had been invited. In addition to the many runners who attended, two managers came. They were essential members of the team and they knew it. That meant a lot to me.

Before completing this chapter I want to elaborate on the running club I started. I founded the club in part because I did not feel my school treated the cross country program with the respect it deserved, either financially or in other ways as well. Whether I was right or wrong in this belief does not matter. I wanted access to funds for extra things when we needed them and the athletic booster club at my school could not help. At least that's what I was told. So, I formed a running club expressly for this purpose.

The club hosted the weekly Prediction Runs during the summer which brought in a little money. The club also organized and promoted a 10k during the town festival just prior to the cross country season. This brought in quite a bit of money. The cross country team worked this race. They were the split timers, the course marshals, the aid station workers, etc. We had a few car washes and things like that, but the 10k was the primary source of funds. Also, funds were sometimes enhanced by contributions. I did not disclose information on that, ever. I'm not sure how the school administrators felt about this club, but I made sure it was all within the rules. Once someone even bought us a brand new digital finish line clock!

The club helped in a variety of ways. Sometimes it provided training shoes or spikes when the kids couldn't afford them, things like that. There is one story I'd like to share that illustrates just how valuable a club like this can be.

My girls had lost an invitational to another team. OK, that will happen sometimes, right? However, in this case, the school had recruited runners from other districts to attend and run there. They got a couple of good ones and it was within the rules because they had left the districts they lived in after their eighth grade year and enrolled as freshmen at their new school. I think they had to pay tuition since they were attending school out of their natural districts, but that really doesn't matter. Anyway, they beat us at an invitational. Given the circumstances surrounding this loss, everyone associated with my program was extremely irritated.

This team won its Sectional and we won ours. So, they were one of the teams at Regional. They soundly defeated us at Regional too. Now we were really upset! I had observed both at the invitational and at the Regional where they beat us that their coaches and fans all were yelling, "Find the green, find the green!" That was us. This went on from the start to the finish at both of these meets. We had to face this team at Semi-State in a week. I wondered, what if we're not green? After checking with the AD, and he with the high school athletic association people, I had one of the girls' mothers, an officer in the running club, go out and buy seven white singlets. This good woman had to look in three or four counties because we needed the tops quickly, they all had to be the same, and they had to meet other requirements also. Some stores had several that met our needs, but not seven. Finally she found seven.

At the Semi-State we kept our warm ups on until immediately before the gun was fired. Then we ripped them off and the race started. The other team never found the green that day or at the State Meet the following week. We got them both times! Not only did we beat them, we really drilled them! The point of this story is that the club gave us a source of funds for something like this when the school could have never even considered it.

There are other organizational things I could describe about my program, but I think that's enough. The configuration of your program could take many forms. It doesn't need to be like mine. But you need to HAVE an organization and YOU need to be organized. To have no system or worse yet, to not be organized personally, is to invite failure.

Chapter 4

The Workouts

Here they come! Here come four and five! We're in great shape. Our one-five gap is less than usual. Come on now, compete! Every place counts! COMPETE! My assistant will get them at about a mile and a half so I can relax just a bit. I'll be at the bottom of the big hill at a little over two miles. They've simply got to be tough there. There is no alternative. I'm running again, but at an easier pace. The way I can cut across here isn't too far.

I never claimed to be a disciple of this coaching guru or that one. Sometimes I read their books, sometimes I didn't. I always had to laugh when another coach, usually a young Hot Shot, would begin talking about training as espoused by this guru or that one. Usually the real purpose behind this type of thing was not to compare ideas about training, but rather to impress you.

I kept training simple. I found what worked and kept it. I'm not sure how I found it anymore, and that really doesn't matter. Some, I am sure, came from my own experience with training. Most, though, probably came from exchanges with other coaches and runners about training. I discussed training with anyone who would. I've been retired for a while now, and I still debate training whenever I have a chance. The guys coaching at my school now have brought their own additions to the training that I taught them. But today it remains basically the same as it was then.

As I mentioned earlier, once the meet season started, we usually had a meet on Tuesday and a meet on Saturday. That left Monday, Wednesday, Thursday (and every now and then we had a meet on Thursday), and Friday. More often than not there were four days a week that we could plan on practicing.

I have always believed meets to be the best practices. We never rested for meets until tourney time, and even then we really didn't approach it as rest. We trained right through them all, although some days were harder than others. I believe what enabled my runners to do this was the summer conditioning. The summer mileage was not terrifically high as you probably noticed, but it was substantial. We were in shape when practice began and from that day on the focus shifted from mileage to quality. I believe in at least a little hard running every day if you want to be good.

What I am going to do now is take you through a typical week. Some of the workouts I'll describe were fixed, that is we did them on that day every week. Others reflect our staple workouts. We did them almost every week but maybe not on the specific day which I assign to them.

Monday was a day to get the "sludge" out of our systems. I never had my kids run on Sundays during the season. I thought one day off was a good thing. After going through the entire warm up routine we always did a Three Minute Drill on Mondays. The goal was simple; see how far you can run in three minutes. We had a circular course 800 meters in length. The start and finish were at the same point. During the Three Minute Drill those who were able to run farther than 800 meters, and that was a lot of them, simply kept going and began a second lap. Either my assistant or I would be out in the middle of the course, sometimes both of us, with watches going, after the start. When the three minutes were up a whistle was blown. We did not call out the running time and had told the kids not to start their watches. They ran until the whistle, not knowing for sure when they could stop. That made it a great mental toughness workout. On the whistle they stopped, got their bearings and either mentally or by some physical means marked where they stopped. Again, we did this every Monday. As the season progressed, so did their marks.

The Three Minute Drill woke us up from the day off. After that we usually did the longest run of the week. This was not as long as the Long Runs during the summer months. Sometimes the boys would run six or seven miles and the girls five or six. The pace of these runs was not closely monitored, but often they could have been called Tempo Runs. We never referred to them by that name, or any other name for that matter. This workout usually ended with one or two Pack 800's.

While we always had ample opportunity to get water, partly due to our excellent managers, we never wasted time with the water excuse. I've seen teams who seem to waste half of their practice time drinking water. If you hydrate during the day, drink when it's appropriate during the workout, and again afterward, you will not dehydrate. My athletes were always instructed to take charge of this themselves and I think they did a good job.

Tuesday was a meet day. We never added any extra miles after the meet besides the cool down mentioned earlier. With the warm up and cool down, meets gave us around five miles, three of which were intense. That is enough. I watched a Hot Shot once, unhappy with his team's performance at an invitational, putting his kids through a workout of 400's on the track right next to where the awards ceremony for the invitational was going on. I quit counting at 15. It made me sick.

Wednesday was the day for the Course Sections workout. This was one thing that we did that no one else was doing. I had gone to a coaches' clinic in Cleveland where I heard a college coach lecture about how he split the course into sections so his athletes had a tool to help with the mental aspect of running a race. As I listened and took notes, I began to think about how I could use this idea. I thought, "I'll take it one step further and turn it into a workout." So Course Sections like most of my other workouts was stolen! Stolen, that is, then enhanced. It's a great workout and besides that, it renders all courses the same. After I describe the workout, you'll see how it also results in all courses getting the same approach. The workout is both physical and mental. Here is the Course Sections handout which the kids received before doing the workout for the first time. It has evolved, so I will show you another form of it right after this one.

Course Sections – Learning to Focus for 5,000 m

1. Starting (400 m)
    Be ready and aggressive.
    Get out fast, but know the line between fast and too fast.
    Don't get boxed in.

2. Positioning (600 m)
    Run further up in the pack than you think is safe.
    Put yourself right on the edge.
    Be closer to the engine than the caboose.

3. Commitment and Concentration (1200 m)
    You've made the commitment in sections 1 and 2 – now you're going to keep it!
    Concentrate on maintaining pace and form as others lose it.
    You must feel like you are working harder just to maintain pace.
    It's human nature to slow down in this stage.

4. Competition (1200 m)
    You are up there and the race is half over – stay there!
    Move up one opponent at a time.
    Think about your responsibility to the team.
    Think about the scoring – passing one opponent is a two point swing.

5. Gut Check (1000 m)
    Nobody feels good in this stage.
    You've thought about this ahead of time – they most likely haven't.
    The light is at the end of the tunnel.
    Go through hell to get to heaven.

6. Finish (600 m)
   Start your finish at the beginning of this stage.
   Use everything you've got left – sprint!
   Think about happy teammates, coaches, parents, etc.

As you can see the 5,000 meter course is split into six sections, each section containing things to understand and think about as you run. Sometimes kids added their own things to think about, but the things you see here are what we gave them. When we did this workout my assistant would take either the boys or girls and I would take the other group. We made a point of switching every week. Both my assistant and I were very mobile at the time so at the start of a section (on our home course), with watch and clipboard in hand, we would remind the runners about the name of the section and what to think about as the section was run. Then we would be at the end of the section before they arrived. Sometimes we had to fudge and start them from a distance but usually we could cut across some way and be there easily. The kids were always instructed to run the course as fast as they could.

When they arrived at the end of a section their times would be recorded. After recording the times, we would make them say what they had been thinking about as they ran. If their thoughts had not been the correct thoughts, we would discuss the whole thing again. The rest between sections was quite long by the time we did everything and we did not time it. We then repeated this process for the next section. After the workout was complete we totaled up the 5k times and reviewed everything with the teams. The first time in a season when we did this workout, the times came very close to the actual times that were run in competition later in the season. Understand now, they were getting five rest intervals in the process. Most times, when we did Course Sections, the runners got faster. Sure, there was an off day every now and then, but not many. The kids were all well aware that we wanted to see progress.

So home meets were usually no contest after doing this workout every week on our course. It yields a tremendous home course advantage. When we went to other courses, though, having done Course Sections repeatedly was nearly as effective. As we toured a course we would pick out landmarks approximating each section. The distances were not really accurate but we made sure the landmarks were clear. My athletes already knew how to approach the course and exactly what to think about each step of the way. It was an advantage.

You might have noticed that the distance for the different sections varied. That's the way it was presented at the clinic where I first learned of this idea. The guys who are coaching at my school now have gone to just having five 1,000 meter sections. I would do something similar now, I think, and basically it's the same thing. I tried this approach with a local runner who wanted help last year and I changed the sections as follows:

Course Sections – Learning to Focus for 5,000 m

1. Starting Stage 500 m
    Be ready and aggressive.
    Get out fast, but know the line between fast and too fast.
    Don't get boxed in.

2. Positioning Stage 1000 m
    Run further up in the pack than you think is safe.
    Put yourself right on the edge.
    Be closer to the engine than the caboose.

3. Commitment and Concentration Stage 1000 m
    You've made the commitment in sections 1 and 2 – now you're going to keep it!
    Concentrate on maintaining pace and form as others lose it.
    You must feel like you are working harder just to maintain pace.
    It's human nature to slow down in this stage.

4. Competition Stage 1000 m
    You are up there and the race is half over – stay there!
    Move up one opponent at a time.
    Think about your responsibility to the team.
    Think about the scoring – passing one opponent is a two point swing.

5. Gut Check Stage 1000 m
    Nobody feels good in this stage.
    You've thought about this ahead of time – they most likely haven't.
    The light is at the end of the tunnel.
    Go through hell to get to heaven

6. Finish Stage 500 m
    Start your finish at the beginning of this stage.
    Use everything you've got left – sprint!
    Think about happy teammates, coaches, parents, etc.
    Think about making YOURSELF happy with a great finish!

When I did this last year we only practiced it a few times. It helped, but it was not the huge advantage that it had been for my kids when we practiced this once a week. One reason I included two versions of this workout is that I have always wondered if there was some significance in the different distances we had in the first version. Some sections were relatively short and some were long. I don't know the answer to that but I do know that when we did this workout the different strengths of each athlete became apparent. Some brought their overall times down by being faster in the shorter sections and some by being faster in the longer sections. The second version pretty well takes that away.

I loved the Course Sections workout and I loved bringing each course into focus by dividing it into sections as we toured it. By the way, whenever possible we would divide a course into sections the day before at practice. When kids had run cross country for a few years they often remembered where the sections were from year to year on a given course. I accumulated a huge file of course maps and would usually have one. If not, I would call well ahead of time and get one. I would also call to see if the course had been changed if I wasn't sure. Usually I knew, though, and my runners would have a map in hand, complete with the Course Sections marked, the day prior to the meet. Then, on the bus traveling to the meet, we would get out the maps and review the course.

That leaves us with Thursday and Friday as the remaining practice days for the week. One of the two days was reserved for Mile Repeats. The other would be used for some variety and would vary from week to week. Let's say, for our purposes here that Thursday was the day for Mile Repeats. The Mile Repeat workout was simple. The miles were run as hard as possible with some forethought. The boys were going to do five and the girls four. They were always reminded to plan ahead. I did not want great variation in the times but I wanted them to run as fast as possible. There would be a three minute rest interval. Again, my assistant took one group, I took the other, and we switched every week.

If the runners finished within 30 seconds of each other we would just start timing the rest interval after the last one. If the mile times varied a lot, we had to adjust. Sometimes groups formed. Every now and then a few runners would be a lot slower than the others. This never bothered me if I felt they were working. I just gave them a shorter distance. I remember one girl whose repeats were 1200 meters and it worked out well. One year I got a little miffed at my boys team and started timing the rest interval when the fastest one finished. They didn't like that and the difference in their times improved. Every now and then we would do one Pack 800 after Mile Repeats but often we would not. Mile Repeats were hard enough and they made us tough.

I had a girls team one year with a big problem. We had three All State caliber athletes, and then a huge two and a half minute gap until four, five, and six came along. Incidentally four, five, and six were always very close together. This puzzled me and aggravated me all season. I had read something about a coach who tied his runners to a rope then had them run hard in order to teach them to run closer as a group. I was desperate. So, I tried it. I got a length of heavy rope about 50 feet long and tied the girls onto it with flag football belts. We ran Mile Repeats this way. My assistant and I were yelling at number one to pull, number two to pull, and number three to pull. They pulled for all they were worth and were having a blast! Numbers four, five, and six ran harder than they ever had before. They were not having fun. Number six would swing way out on the corners due to the centrifugal force but no one fell. We did the entire workout this way. Next meet the gap between number three and the rest was less than a minute and the gap between one and six was about a minute and a half. We had a much better team. For a long time that year I took the rope to practice and would lay it down in plain sight just to remind them. I never had to use it again. The guys who are coaching at my school now told me that when they got the job one of the first things the AD told them was that they could not do the rope workout.

That leaves Friday as the last practice day of the week since Saturday was a meet day. Friday became a time for variety. Early in my coaching this was frequently a game of some sort. Then, as my kids became more serious athletes, I kind of got away from that. Once the captain of the boys team asked if we could stop playing games. "We just want to train," he said. I knew I was getting somewhere then. There is, however, a place for games and I never totally quit using them. There are whole books on these kinds of activities and I'll leave it to you to get your own source, but over the years we had scavenger hunts, marker runs, poker runs, all kinds of games. Some teams liked them more than others.

Fridays could also see another workout that we did frequently, Indian File Running. The name of this workout is probably no longer politically correct so you might have to change it. I would put the runners in groups according to pace. Each group was given a time in which to cover our 5k home course. It goes like this. The group is in a straight line, about two strides apart, and the assigned pace is established. The person at the back of the group sprints to the front, raises his/her hand to signal, and the person now last repeats the process. This is a good workout unless the group pace is too slow or the sprints are not hard. My assistant and I monitored both the group pace and the speed of the sprints closely. At the end of practice on Fridays we would almost always do one or two Pack 800's.

Saturday was another meet day and we would repeat the process the following week. If I sensed that my teams were having difficulty, I would adjust. You've got to. But you must NOT be afraid to push your athletes. Fatigue is always a part of hard training. After a few years of coaching I realized that my assistant and I could pretty well determine if our kids were starting to get too tired. As long as they came to practice chattering about school and complaining about their teachers and classes, we knew they were all right. If it was quiet as they arrived, they could be getting too tired. About once a season, usually on a Friday, I would surprise the teams by directing them to do the cool down right after they had completed the warm up. Practice was over! They would look at me like they thought I had gone crazy, but they always came back the next day fired up and ready to go. I chose those days very, very carefully.

We never did any weight training. I suppose that pumping iron has a place in training to be a distance runner, but I don't think that place is at the high school level. Becoming runners is enough of a task at this age. Let the weight training go as the final polish some college coach can give them. I think some high school cross country coaches, usually Hot Shots, try to include weights as a part of their approach because they think it will impress someone. To me it's just wasting time that could be used for running.

There were other things that we did every now and then, but basically I considered all of them to be variations of the workouts I have reported. I do know, without doubt, that my athletes liked having the routine and knowing what to expect in practice. Most days they knew what they would be doing and didn't have to ask. We never ran repeats of any distance other than the Mile Repeats. I will add that we kept records of every Mile Repeat and Course Sections workout. Doing this afforded us more opportunities to provide feedback and reward progress.

My observation is that coaches who are too "easy" on their runners far outnumber those who are too "hard" on them. The quickest way to turn kids off is to have them go home feeling that their work was not significant. I always refer to this as feeling "like they didn't get their money's worth." Don't be afraid to take it right up to the line. You'll know when you approach it if you are paying attention. Just know your athletes and communicate with them.

Chapter 5

Dealing With Injuries

OK, I made it in plenty of time. I'm here at the bottom of the hill, a little more than two miles in. If I've done my job all year this is where they'll really test themselves, find out if they've got the guts to see it through. Number one and two are past, still flying. They'll be fine. Where's three? Can't afford to fall off at all. OK, OK. Three isn't too bad. Come on, WORK! I'll stay here until four and five come. Can't let them get lost. Points pile up in a hurry where they're at. My assistant is about a quarter mile ahead, on the other side of the hill.

I've seen situations over the years on some teams where some kids almost never practiced because they were "injured." Usually those who are not practicing are a fatal distraction to a team. In my first year I was faced with this very thing. So I'll begin there.

The first year I coached probably half my team sat out half the time. I was a runner so I knew what was going on. They weren't injured; they either ached somewhere a bit and wanted to take it easy for a few days, or just plain wanted to take it easy. It was very frustrating and it was part of the conversation I had with my assistant when he told me I had to take charge. Whose fault was it that this situation occurred? It was mine. I was reluctant to face this issue in the forthright manner it demands.

There were several things I had not done. I had not educated them about the difference between an ache or pain and an injury. And just as importantly, I had not given them enough of a sense of the magnitude of their endeavor. If young people feel what they are doing is significant they will try very hard to disregard the usual and typical pains associated with running. After that first year I spent a lot of coach's talks defining what a real injury was and even more communicating why their efforts were so terribly urgent.

Somewhere during my second season my runners quit complaining about being injured and decided to get something done. From that point on I remember only two real injuries and, looking back from my current vantage point, very little of the trivial complaining about being injured that dominates the scene on many teams. I remember reading somewhere that the best way to handle a complaint of this nature is to listen sympathetically and ignore it. I gave them more. I gave my athletes education and pride.

What do you do if a kid comes to practice and says Mom said not to run? I encountered this several times early in my coaching. Mom isn't coaching the team, you are. Tell him or her to run! If Mom really said that, she'll call you and you can clear up what constitutes an injury and why it is crucial to practice. What if a runner brings a note from a doctor? Well, that directive must be followed, by both the runner and you. That is why it is vital to educate your athletes before these problems begin. There are many, many kids who want to be "part of a team" but really do not want to work. When these kids see where you are coming from they will either change or realize they are not meant to run cross country. The notion of kids quitting bothered me early in my coaching, but really, how can you quit something you never truly started? You shouldn't be on the cross country team if you don't want to run.

I'll give you my take on doctors. What's the surest cure for a repetition injury such as running might produce? Rest is the easy answer. The family doctor will very often prescribe exactly that. What does rest do? It will heal you if you are injured and take away your season at the same time. If you are not really injured it will just take away your season.

Early in my coaching, during the time I was faced with a lot of injury complaints, some of my runners took to hanging around the school's training room. They would go there looking for sympathy and very often would get it. I noticed this, met with the team, and directed them not to go into the training room without my permission. The athletic trainer heard about this and was very angry. I guess I don't blame her, but I did what I had to do. I was in charge of my team.

How do you know the difference between a real injury, one that needs to be dealt with before you go on, and a fake or imagined injury? First of all, know that you have educated your athletes on this matter. Then, know your runners. Make an effort to learn what makes them tick. If the complaint persists, and it is from an educated, motivated athlete, then listen. The development of sports medicine has taken the sting out of sending kids to the doctor. Just make sure they go to a sports medicine specialist. If they go to the old family doctor, their season will likely be over.

I had a girl on the team once who developed a hitch in her stride about mid season. It remained and became more and more pronounced until it got to the point where it was a very plain limp. If I asked her about it she would just shrug it off. And, it did not seem to show up when she was running hard. I let it go unaddressed for quite a while. One day at practice, watching the warm up, I noticed that she was limping so badly she could hardly jog. I called her over and told her to take the next three days off, just go home, catch up on homework, and recharge. I had in mind that after the three days she would return and we would see how her limp was. She went home.

That evening my phone rang. It was Dad, very angry, calling to report that his daughter was at home crying, wondering why I kicked her out of practice. He coached baseball and JV basketball at another school so he had some knowledge in these matters. I told him that I had not kicked his daughter out, but that I had told her to leave because her limp was so bad she could hardly warm up. He began to soften a bit in his approach, but wondered why I had not taken the time to explain to her in more detail why I was sending her home. Maybe I should have. I pointed out to him that I did not want to make a big deal out of it at practice because I did not want to start an epidemic by showing too much sympathy in front of the other girls. He then revealed that he'd been trying to help her manage the injury for over a month. "OK," I said, "it's time to go to the doctor."

He took his daughter to a sports medicine doctor who found a stress fracture in her shin. This was a real injury and needed to be dealt with. She returned to practice after her doctor's appointment. I told the team that she would be coming to practice, but not running while she healed. This girl was our number four runner and the tournament was starting soon. I explained that she would probably not be able to return to the level that made her number four, but that she would run in the State Meet if she felt she could, and wanted to, as number seven. They understood, and she ran as number seven. She's on a relatively short list of girls in the state's history who ran in the State Meet all four years of high school.

The fastest boy I ever coached also had a stress fracture. This one played out quite differently. We had completed the first two weeks of practice and the first meet was coming up the next day. My phone rang that evening shortly after practice. It was the boy's mother calling from the doctor's office to say that her son had his foot in a cast due to a stress fracture. I talked with the boy. He said, "Coach, do something." I spoke with the doctor and asked him a few questions. It was obvious that he did not want to talk. He was upset that I questioned him, I guess. I asked Mom if she would consider getting a second opinion. She said she had complete faith in this guy. Six weeks in a cast. Well, there you have it!

This boy did not miss a day of practice. He was the captain so he still had a function on the team. He would charge around at practice yelling at the guys, kind of hopping and running at the same time, on the cast that encased his entire foot.

After a month I called Dad and suggested that he take the boy to a sports medicine doctor and have the foot reexamined. He wondered if I was saying the first doctor was a quack. "Well, no," I said, "but maybe it's healed fast and getting a different opinion might be good." He made an appointment, they saw a sports medicine specialist, and the boy was back running the day after the appointment.

After more than a month off it was a difficult comeback. One of my favorite memories centers on the Conference Meet. After being cleared to run, I had this boy run JV at one invitational just to see how the foot would do. I told him to run about 18 minutes, not to push at all. He was a 16 minute runner so 18 was an easy pace for him. He did it and the foot felt fine. Following that we had a regular season meet with another school in our conference. I told the boy, "Just run number four for us today." He did and helped us defeat one of the teams that would be a challenger in the upcoming Conference Meet. I'm not sure the other team even knew he had run. They were used to seeing him at number one.

The Conference Meet arrived and my guy was still not in shape. What he did that day was astounding. He placed fourth individually in this eight team Conference Meet. He was in pain with a terrible side ache much of the race but never once looked at me for any sympathy. He was too busy racing. I really hated it when kids looked at me begging for sympathy as they raced. It was one of the most impressive performances I have seen at the high school level. Several opposing coaches had written him off for the year and seemed almost resentful that he had run and placed so well. One even went so far as to suggest that the conference should require athletes to run at least half of the regular season meets before being eligible to compete in the Conference Meet.

Learning how to deal with the real/imagined/fake injury was one of the things that I had to learn in order to become a COACH. It took a couple of years. When athletes understand and recognize that aches and pains are to be expected, that's a big step. Then when they develop pride in what they are accomplishing, this pride becomes greater than any ache or pain that could develop short of a true injury and that simply does not come up very often.

Chapter 6

Building Tradition

Here they come! Here come four and five! We're in good shape and there's less than a mile to go. Come on, be tough! Gut check! GUT CHECK!! I think maybe I see number six coming in the distance. Boy, if that's six, that'd be a bonus. But, I can't stay. I'm running now, toward the finish. I won't get into the huge crowd. I'll be at about two and three quarter miles. My assistant will be close to that point too. That way we can yell and maybe be heard. But I've got to run harder. Otherwise I'll miss number one.

When I began coaching my school had no cross country tradition. Well maybe I'm wrong. We might have had one tradition, but it was not the right kind. Toward the end of my first season, with the Sectional, the first step in our State Tournament coming up, the AD told me that he sure wished us good luck over there at the park where the Sectional was held, but that our school's teams had never run well there and probably never would. The tradition was to go to the Sectional and be done for the year. We went to the Sectional that year and we were done for the season just like tradition dictated.

In the following years I made sure we adopted this course as a second home course. We even hosted a home meet on that course once. After all, it was a public park. Often in my third and maybe even fourth season the team would meet outside the school, make sure everyone had a ride, and then head to that park for practice. My assistant and I drove but, yes, kids drove too. Looking back on that I can say for sure that creating this situation was not one of the smartest or safest things I have done. Well, the AD caught wind of this and put a stop to it. I don't blame him for that! Sometimes if we had a Saturday practice, or if there was a no school day for some reason, we would still meet at the park and practice. We really did turn that course into a second home. In the 20 plus years since the AD mentioned the tradition of not running well at this park my school has won close to 90% of the Sectional Meets.

The organization of my program, the workouts, the athletes, the victories, and the defeats all became part of our catalog of traditions. One tradition that developed within a few years was that of having Mile Repeats be the workout at the first practice. The runners looked forward to this all summer, both with trepidation and excitement. They knew it would be hard, but they also knew it was the first step in finding out how they measured up against others. The Course Sections workout, the Three Minute Drill, and others set standards that became traditional. Often you would hear someone say something like this, "Fletcher got all the way over there (pointing) at almost 1100 meters last year in a Three Minute Drill!" These things just happened. My athletes knew I was extremely impressed by effort and production and they learned to share this.

Some traditions, like many of my other coaching tools, I stole. The football coach was my assistant in track. He was new to the school and he brought with him some very good methods. I had observed that his players sometimes huddled up at practice and loudly yelled the word, "Pride." I asked him about it. He said that "P was for performance, R was for respect, I was for integrity, D was for determination, and E was for edification. The last one, he stated, often had to be defined. I remember I didn't let him know that I thought cross country athletes were smarter than football players. I asked if we could use the PRIDE cheer in track and cross country. He was flattered and we did. I'm not sure that the acronym still exists, but cross country still does their "Pride" cheer to this day before meets. We used to do it frequently also at tough points in a hard practice, say, after three repeats in the Mile Repeat workout (two remaining) or at Gut Check section in the Course Section workout. So, I stole that one, with permission.

The girls took this a step further. I think it originated with two highly creative girls that were on the team. They decided that after a meet, they would start doing what they called a "Foot Pride."

I'll do my best to describe it, but neither my assistant nor I really ever mastered the whole thing although we were often drafted into trying to do it. The Foot Pride went like this. The girls team sat in a circle. (The boys probably would have been stymied at this point if they had tried it because boys don't seem to be able to do things like sit in a nice circle.) Anyway, the girls made a perfect circle, sitting on the ground, feet pointing toward the center. Then they would start.

"P, P, P, R, I,
I, I, I, D, E,
P, R, I,
I, D, E,
P, R, I, D, E,
Pride!"

They would rhythmically chant this at the tops of their voices, and then launch into other things that I never really understood. Anyway, it was complete with hand clapping and foot movement. After a meet I would stand back, usually after we had just drilled opponents, and watch my team do this, and then I would watch the other teams watching us. What a feeling!

Remember the sports writer I mentioned earlier? The one who had been giving us coverage before all the others? Well, he responded to a comment I made on Facebook the other day saying that he was watching the girls team "doing that foot thing you taught them 20 years ago." This would have been after their Sectional victory this year. But, I am afraid that, in the interest of honesty, I must admit that I did not teach it to them. I couldn't even do it.

Not all traditions came out of positive situations. There's one in particular that I would like to describe. This happened in my second or third year of coaching. We were getting better at that time, but had not arrived at the level of excellence we would get to in the near future. It was the Conference Meet. I had this guy on my team named Blough. Blough was a very good runner and he had a chance to be All Conference. The top 10 at this meet are automatically All Conference and five more are elected. With about 800 meters left in the race, Blough was running in sixth place. At that point on the course runners turned into the woods before emerging with about 300 meters left to the finish. Blough went into the woods in sixth place and came out in 18th place. What? "What happened?" I asked as he came through the finish chute. "I had to pee," he answered. I was speechless. When the coaches began voting for the five additional All Conference spots, one asked if I wanted to say anything on Blough's behalf. "Please don't vote for him," was all I could muster.

This spot on the Conference Meet course became known as "Blough's Woods." This course was the same as the Sectional and Regional course so this tradition served triple duty. The course has changed a bit and today Blough's Woods is no longer part of it. In the years after this event all of my kids knew this as Blough's Woods and I would often hear coaches and runners from other schools referring to it by that name as well. Nobody ever stopped to pee again.

While I am on the topic of naming things I would encourage you to give as many names to as many places on as many courses as you can. On various courses in the State tournament series we had the Tunnel of Trees, the Land of the Slogs, the 10-Step Tree, the Cornfield, the Woodpile, the S-Curves, and others. And, oh yes, Blough's Woods.

Still another tradition was the Friday evening pasta meal before the big Saturday meet. We would usually go, after practice, to one of the runner's homes, where a pasta and salad feast had been prepared. Sometimes the coaches hosted these also. They were fun and these types of traditions go a long, long way toward establishing a true feeling of team among the kids, parents, and coaches.

Sometimes after the Sectional or Regional teams would "TP" the coach. Of course the coach acted like he hated it, but really, he enjoyed it. One year, one of the mothers and the girls team were caught by a cop as they were "TPing" my house. He brought them to the door and I had to say it was OK. I remember acting extremely unhappy for awhile before letting them off the hook.

One of our finest traditions was the post season hayride. It was complete with a huge John Deere tractor and a trailer piled high with bales of hay. Everyone would come to one of the parent's houses, enjoy a huge potluck meal, and then the kids would leave on the hayride with one parent driving and a few others on the trailer. The rest of us either sat in a garage or around a campfire visiting. After the hayride, cross country season was officially over.

Some kids have told me in the years since that it was good that I did not go on the hayride.

Things as trivial as where we camped when we went to invitationals became traditions. We were always one of the very first teams to arrive, which I guess could be considered a tradition in itself, but with no direction from the coaches, runners would get off the bus when we arrived at an invitational and proceed directly to the same spot year after year. They do this even now.

Some traditions seem to just develop. Others need a boost to get started, then they take off on their own. Still others must be manufactured. But for all types of traditions, you need to recognize the potential, then provide the foundation for them to stand on. Look around and simply pick something to start with. You'll be surprised at how quickly and totally kids latch onto things. You can never have too much tradition.

Chapter 7

Enjoying the Kids

I see my assistant about 100 meters up the course. I'll stay right here and get them. Got to have a strong finish at State. Otherwise you'll give a lot of points away. Here they come. FINISH! FINISH! FINISH! There's nothing else now. Nothing's left but to finish! Nobody looks strong now. None of them is smooth. If you've really raced, you are shot. I want my runners to be shot and they know it. But they also know they've got to find it, find that finish sprint. We've practiced it enough. I told them all year that the best practices start AFTER you're real tired! I hear my assistant yelling now and from here it looks like we are passing people. Could it be?

If you don't enjoy being with young people you can't possibly be a COACH. You might be a Hot Shot, or a Custodial Coach, or even a Lifer. You might graduate from one of those categories to another, but you will never become a COACH. In this chapter I am going to present a few stories, ones I haven't told yet, about some of my kids. They shared the enjoyment of a very intense activity with me and I remain friends with many of them today. I thoroughly enjoyed the time I had with them in cross country. They knew it.

Mitch

In my first year of coaching I had many boys on the team and all of them were slow. One boy in particular named Mitch stands out in my memories of this team. Mitch routinely ran the meets in 23 or 24 minutes. He never missed practice, or was a problem in any way, but he never really worked all that hard either. My assistant and I frequently tried to figure out what benefit kids like Mitch were getting from being on the team. We could really come up with nothing.

In my second year Mitch stayed after practice one day. Runners would do this often, especially when there was something they wanted to talk about. As Mitch cleared his throat, I noticed the tears in his eyes. "What's the problem, Mitch," I asked. He explained that his dad had recently lost his job and that Mitch had an offer from a family friend to work for him after school on a regular basis. Mitch needed to make money to help his family. "I've got to quit cross country," he said. He added, "I want you to know that I really like being on the team and I really like running." Before he was done he was sobbing. We talked more about it and Mitch left that day. He graduated in the spring and I never had another chance to visit with him.

I do know this. Mitch taught me that kids get things out of their activities that we adults don't understand. I'm not sure what Mitch was gaining from his participation, but there was something. It was significant to him. Mitch also taught me that kids like him should be valued as team members.

Jon

Jon was a member of the cross country team all four of his high school years. He was a 19 or 20 minute runner. Jon was also in the marching band so his time was in demand. He made it work and even though he missed a few meets here and there for band activities, he also missed a few band events for meets, always being proactive to be in accordance with school policy. Jon would work pretty hard. He usually looked like he hated it, but he did what was asked of him. By the time I retired Jon was already out of college and law school. He had a job in a high powered law firm in a big city.

They had a little ceremony for me at the school after a basketball game, more of a roast than anything, when I retired. Jon's dad came. I hadn't seen him or Jon for six or seven years so it was quite flattering and a real surprise. Dad reported that Jon had been planning to come for this event, but that something at work had come up and he had called to make sure his dad came in his place. Jon had written something that he wanted his dad to read. Dad's turn at the microphone came and he began reading. Jon went on and on about how he always dreaded a certain workout because he knew I'd be at the top of the hill looking at him and yelling as he ran up. He said that sometimes, as he was approaching the point where he knew I'd be, he'd visualize me as Hitler standing on the hilltop, and other times as Satan himself. Well, Jon went on to say that he understood why I always yelled at him. He remembered. One of the things he remembered most vividly was that I would yell, "Jon, how are you going to ever race somebody if you don't practice it?" He concluded by saying something like this, "Coach, I want you to know I still run. I run to relieve my stress. I save my racing for work. When the negotiations get tough I always see you on top of that hill, yelling at me, and I think, yes coach, I'm racing now."

I think that is one of the best compliments I have ever received.

Jolene

I mentioned Jolene before as the fasted girl I ever coached. But, I haven't told this story yet. It was Sectional time. The tournament was going to begin tomorrow. My assistant and I finished preparing the team to do its best that Friday evening at practice, and then we sent them home. The bus was leaving at 7:00 AM. Some were always last minute, but most were pretty good about being on time, and Jolene was never late.

She didn't show up. Seven o'clock came and went. I would usually wait a few minutes but sometimes we left runners behind. Ten minutes passed. I knew something must be wrong. There were no cell phones at this time so I sent my assistant into the school to call Jolene's home. By chance he caught someone. Jolene had been in a car accident on the way to meet us at the school. She had run into someone who was backing out of a driveway. Jolene was OK and her mom said they would meet us at the park where the meet was held.

We arrived and Jolene was there waiting for us. She seemed somewhat shaken but otherwise all right. "Do you want to run?" I asked. "That's why I'm here," she smiled. "OK," I responded, and that was that. She ran and won the meet. The team won also. After the meet I learned the car had been totaled. I remember this surprised me. I had envisioned a fender bender of some sort. I drove past the shop where the car was on my way home and it really was totaled. It was bad. A lot of descriptive words come to mind, words like resilient, dedicated, and committed, but none really do Jolene justice.

She was not only fast; she was also tougher than nails!

Ryan

As a student in middle school I had him in math class. Ryan was one of those students who did his homework pretty much when he felt like it. But he was a good person. One time I had to threaten to take him out of some middle school meets if he didn't start doing his math. He responded appropriately.

Another time, during Ryan's freshman year, he ran a particularly bad race. The effort was very poor. Now this guy was going to be a good runner and I wanted to get rid of this minimal effort tendency as fast as I could. He was on the small side, and smooth, real smooth. So after practice one day I told him to stay. I drove my truck along side of him while he ran and I lectured him every step of the way. I think it was around 10 miles that he ran and I was not really saying a lot of positive things. As we were finishing up I looked at him and said, "And go get a haircut, will you!" I am still in touch with Ryan and I see him every now and then. The haircut thing has become a joke between us since my hair in retirement is usually longer than his is now.

Going into Ryan's senior year he had never broken 17 minutes. He ran consistently in the low 17's, but never under. I really wanted him to and he really wanted to. Now I knew that Ryan thought my daughter was cute so one day I told him if he broke 17 I'd set him up on a date with my daughter. Well, he did. I was going to deliver, but since we had made the agreement Ryan had gotten a girlfriend and he was no longer footloose and fancy free. Sorry, you missed your chance.

Ryan is one of the coaches at my old school now.

Tony

Tony was one of the captains. He was a rock solid mid 17 minute runner who absolutely made the most of his natural ability. Tony was not smooth, he had a short choppy stride, and his arms flailed in circles as he ran. I admired what Tony got out of himself.

One Tuesday we had a crucial regular season conference meet with a team that was going to be a real problem for us. Tony ran about 20 minutes that day and we lost. I was beside myself. What in the world had happened to our captain? "Tony," I yelled. "Get over here!" He quickly ran over, head hanging. "What happened?" I demanded. "Well, coach," he began, "the other kids were giving blood at school today." "So you gave blood? On the day of a meet?" "Yeah coach," he replied, "they had sandwiches and I was hungry."

I think maybe I muttered a few bad words before walking away. But Tony was a great asset to the team and a great guy to be around.

David

David was going to be a freshman. We had started practice and were in the two week span of time between when we could start and when school started. Those who could usually drove to these practices, some parents brought their kids, and a few runners rode their bikes. The bikes were parked in a small cluster of trees near the center point of the course and I parked my truck there too. We were doing the Course Sections workout. It's a hard workout for anyone, but it's really hard for a freshman who has never done this type of thing before. David was a good sized boy, long and lanky but with a smooth stride, thinly disguised in adolescent clumsiness.

We were running the Gut Check Section. This is just a little over half way through the workout, at its toughest point. I was at the end of the section waiting to talk with them about the section and record their times. One by one they arrived and I took care of the business. Then it hit me. David wasn't there. What? Was he hurt? What happened? "Well, coach," someone offered, "we were going past the trees and David just ran over and jumped on his bike and took off."

After practice I went to David's home and visited with him. He returned to practice the next day and went on to have a very good four year cross country career.

Nicole

Nicole was our sixth runner for four years. She was Junior Miss in our state and was involved in about anything the school offered that had to do with music or drama. Nicole was a hard worker, and by the time she got to high school, she had a tremendous balancing act to make all her different activities work.

I remember one day when Nicole was a sixth grader I decided to speak to the middle school teams. I think it might have been one of their last days of practice for the season. This was early in my coaching and I remember as I told them that someday it might be possible for them to run in the State Meet, Nicole was looking up at me with these incredibly bright eyes, just soaking up every word. She ran in the State Meet in three of her high school years.

Here's what I really wanted to say about Nicole. As the sixth runner she did not really count in the scoring. That is, unless the score was tied. Well, twice in Nicole's career, which was also during the time of our long regular season winning streak, the score was tied and Nicole was the tiebreaker. We won both of those meets due to our sixth runner, Nicole. She ran hard, as if she was going to count in the score, every meet.

She runs marathons today.

Dan

Dan was extremely talented. Running came naturally to him. He had a long, long stride and he was very strong besides. My team that wound up finishing fourth at State had needed one more runner to get to that level. Dan developed into that runner. At the State Meet that year he was the second best sophomore in the state. I had been involved in a number of parent/student/coach/teacher/guidance counselor meetings related to Dan so I was well aware of potential problems.

After we finished fourth at State, Dan disappeared. Back in that day I ran with the kids who were not in other sports after school in the off season. But Dan never showed up. The other guys never seemed to know anything about where he might be. I learned that Dan had gotten into trouble with the law. He had been expelled from school. Dan was allowed to return to school the next fall, but he was ineligible to compete on the cross country team. He could practice with us but he could not compete. Dan came to every practice and worked hard. He would be way out in front in every workout, but according to school policy, he could not compete. It bothered me a lot, not the school policy, just the fact that he had taken himself out of the picture.

Dan disappeared again after his junior year. He never ran another meet after being the second best sophomore in the state. One day six or seven years later Dan appeared in the doorway of my classroom. He came in and we had a good, long visit. We chatted about running, of course, but he also told me that he'd spent some time in prison and was trying to make a new start. Dan was going to be married soon, he said, and he had a good job.

I'd like to see Dan again and I wonder how he is doing.

Tara

We were on the starting line at the State Meet. Seven girls were nervously stomping around in our assigned box. We had completed the entire warm up and pre-race routine. The starter was giving final instructions. Like all State Meets this one had a huge crowd on hand.

Tara was our fifth runner. At the State Meet the fifth runner is critical in the scoring. You need everyone to perform well, but at number five the race is extremely crowded. If number five is off a little the points really pile up in a hurry, more than one per second.

As all these things were going through my head and the start of the race was moments away, Tara looked at me. "Coach," she said, "I've got to pee." I told her it was too late and she stated it again, with great emphasis. "OK, girls, make a circle," I instructed. They did, backs to the inside of the circle, and Tara took care of business right there on the line.

I remember thinking, "We're really ready." We were. We placed sixth and were probably no better than the 10th best team there. Tara ran a great race.

Another Ryan

Ryan was an extraordinarily fine, upstanding young man. This was Ryan's senior season and he was one of the two captains.

Shortly before the tournament started a couple of the guys took a short cut on one of the Friday runs. I overheard the two captains conversing about it and moved in to address the issue. I was going to take care of it. The captains asked if they could handle it. "OK," I said. As I moved away I heard Ryan admonishing the two boys who had shortened the course. He was not using socially acceptable language. It was the only time I ever heard him use what would generally be considered inappropriate words. I smiled inside, confident that the correct message was being delivered.

It was the same year and I think it was the week of the State Meet, either that or Semi-State. The AD came out as we were finishing practice. It was never a good thing to see the AD coming out to practice. He walked up to me and said, "Coach, we have a problem. I don't know if you noticed this morning when you came to school, but last night all the stop signs on the school property were stolen. We have reason to believe that the signs are in Ryan's garage. Now, the principal and I will overlook this if the signs are returned before I get to school tomorrow." There were about 15 missing signs.

I thanked him and he left. I called the boys team together and told them about the signs. I could see Ryan and a few others looking at each other as I spoke. "Boys," I said, "if those signs are returned before the AD gets to school tomorrow, there is no problem. If the signs are not returned, they have reason to believe that cross country is responsible, and the State Meet is probably down the drain." The next morning there were 15 stop signs at the entrance by which the AD always entered the building.

Nothing more was really ever said about this but I was always very glad the AD and principal saw fit to handle it this way.

Bloomski

No one called Bloomski by his real name. The football coach had given him this nickname in track and it just stuck. I don't have one particular story about Bloomski. Maybe there were so many I can't sort one out, or perhaps there simply weren't any. At any rate, no account of the kids I coached would be complete without mentioning Bloomski.

In track he tried pole vaulting. Day after day he tried vaulting and I don't think he ever cleared a height. None. He tried sprinting. He was slow. Finally we put Bloomski in the 800. This was good. Here he could participate and not embarrass himself. He ran 800 in around 2:25 – 2:30. One day he told me he was going to run cross country in the fall. Oh my! He and his parents came to the spring meeting, they took the Summer Training Program home, and Bloomski trained. I had no idea what to expect but I did see him a number of times at the Prediction Runs or on Thursdays. He always seemed to be working hard.

When we started practice it became obvious that Bloomski was much improved. "Hey, he's not going to be too bad," I remember saying to my assistant. Bloomski was a little heavy set, but he had slimmed down a bit over the summer. He was a fairly tall guy but ran with a very short stride. In no way was Bloomski a natural runner. Bloomski went on to run two years of cross country and was consistently in the mid 17's.

He used to stop by to visit regularly after he graduated, while I was still teaching. I remember once he told me he had started smoking. I chewed him out for that. I miss seeing Bloomski.

Stacey

Stacey was our number five runner for three years. She was a short girl and was a smooth little runner. Stacey was slower than the four girls in front of her. We had four All-State caliber athletes on the team, then Stacey. Every season Stacey was faced with the same situation. How was she going to become a good enough number five to, first of all, get us to State and then be an effective number five at State?

Going into her sophomore year Stacey must have felt a lot of pressure. She came to me after one of the first practices to say that she had to quit. She had to quit, she told me, to spend more time reading the Bible. That's a difficult one to debate. My assistant and I tried to reason with her for over an hour. Finally we gave up and went home. I called Stacey's mother that evening and she assured me that Stacey would return. Stacey did.

Stacey was well aware of what she needed to do. It was simple. She needed to work hard, real hard, all season long. Then she would get to where she had to be. And, every year she did. One year, the year my girls were second at State, Stacey finished only one or two places behind number four.

That's what cross country is all about!

Mary

Mary never ran in middle school. But I taught there and she was in my math class her eighth grade year. I don't think she participated in sports at the middle school level. One spring day, toward the end of Mary's eighth grade year, I told her I thought she should think about being a member of the cross country team in high school.

Mary looked at me and asked, "Does the school furnish the skis?"

I told Mary that this sport involved running, not skiing. She came out for cross country and ran all four of her high school years. She was a good, dependable runner on a good team.

Mary, now in her upper 30's, ran a half marathon this year.

I am sure that if my former athletes ever got started they could come up with some very amusing and strange stories about me. Probably at least as many as I can tell about them. I could add many, many more stories about my runners, but you get the point. We were on the same team and we enjoyed each other. If you are going to be a COACH there is no substitute for truly enjoying your kids; none. You must enjoy even the things that drive you nuts. There is no way you can succeed if you don't like being around them.

I taught school for 32 years and coached for more than 20. I can honestly say that my memories of these years are dominated by my cross country runners. As a COACH you have the opportunity to open doors for and with these kids, doors that can only be opened in a team setting. My advice is to enjoy them, recognizing that your role as COACH offers a unique opportunity to contribute to their development.

Chapter 8

The Finish Line

I'm cold, my fingers are numb. But I'm warm at the same time. My kids have all finished now and they keep asking me how we did. It's impossible to say right away in a meet as big as the State Meet so I just tell them I'm not sure. I think we did a great job, but I won't say it yet. We'll find out soon. Parents have formed a group behind our camp. The manager is giving sweats back to the runners. Hey! Put those sweats on. I don't care if you're not cold. Put them on! Then get the cool down started. Hugs and smiles are being exchanged. And yes, there are tears also, some of joy and some of fatigue or apprehension. My assistant is smiling. He thinks we did well too.

I've tried to detail the program we developed. I say "we" because that is who developed it. Our program came into existence with the collaborative effort of coaches, athletes, and parents. All of these people played a role. I realize that I have previously referred to "my program." In a sense it was mine because the philosophy, the organization, and the training originated with me. But in another very real sense, it belonged to all of us. While the coaches and athletes were directly involved in the competition, success in that competition could not have happened without the support of parents. The program simply could not have developed as it did without everyone's involvement.

As coaches, my assistant and I set the tone and created the environment in which the others could respond. Athletes responded to the organization, the training, and the coaching techniques that were offered. Parents responded to the same factors, encouraged their kids, supported the coaches, but almost never applied too much pressure to either their kids or the coaches.

Among the program's successes are many runners who went on to have collegiate careers, NAIA as well as all divisions of the NCAA. A number of athletes from this program have gone on to become coaches in their own right. While some have produced highly visible achievements in their competitions, others have worked quietly, enhancing the sport of cross country from elementary school through the collegiate levels. Perhaps the truest measure of the program's success is revealed in the high percentage of athletes who have continued to be runners as the years go by. Parents and kids who were involved in our program have treasured memories as do the coaches.

Our program had a lot more than its share of competitive accomplishments. Among them are many Conference, Sectional and Regional titles, as well as five consecutive girls Semi-State championships. The Semi-States happened in my last five years of coaching and I'm very proud of that. In addition the boys finished fourth at State one year and in my last six years the girls team finished fourth, second, fifth, third, sixth, and 13th. Since my coaching years the boys team has won a State title and finished very high at State almost every season. The girls team has added another State runner up finish to the program resume and has produced equally as many high finishes at State as the boys. And remember, two of my former runners direct the program now. I am as proud of their tenure as I am of mine.

All of this and more has been accomplished in a state where there is no class system. My school had fewer than 800 students when I started coaching and we competed with schools having more than 3,500 students. Today my school is a bit larger but the disparity in school size between my school and some of their competitors remains the same.

I hope you noticed the lack of training jargon in my description of the program. Was the training sound? You bet it was. But, there was no mention of Vo2 Max, LT running, or any other scientific training terminology. Kids don't want to or need to know those terms. We didn't even use terms such as lactic acid, aerobic, anaerobic or anything else like that. Rather, the training was always characterized in relation to the amount of work it required; hard work and even harder work. The runners identified with it and adopted it as their own. They learned that hard work would make them good and even harder work would make them better.

Everything we did was sound from a training perspective but I take even more pride in the fact that everything we did was sound from an educational and a human relations point of view. Athletes, coaches, and parents were all on the same team.

As you make the journey toward becoming a COACH think about the things I've tried to help you understand. Take these ideas and methods, make them your own, and change them to fit your situation. But don't waste valuable time in the Custodial, Hot Shot, or Lifer categories of coaching. Recognize these phases and keep learning until you arrive at the place that only about 10% of us ever reach. You'll know it when you get there.

I hear parents and kids cheering now. Team scores are up and we did better than any of us could have hoped. You can't ask for more than that. I'm not cold at all now. The principal comes over, shakes my hand. He does that every year but I still wonder if he knows what this is all about or why he hired me. Everyone's yelling, congratulations are offered from every angle. I'm elated. But I'm a little let down at the same time. Our big day is over and now we have a whole year to wait to find out if we can get even better. Runners are stretching. Then we'll go over to the awards stand. It's been a long time since I started coaching but not quite that long since I learned to COACH. And I know exactly how I got here.

Made in the USA
Lexington, KY
25 June 2019